SHAPING A THEOLOGICAL MIND

Rarely do theological thinkers have the opportunity to present their own self-understanding of both their context and their methodology and the inter-relation of the two. This book gives leading theological minds from North America, Great Britain and Europe an opportunity to explore the shaping of their theological minds in regard to context and methodology. Asking 'why theology', each contributor explores their sense of call to the Christian faith, the purpose of their theological journey, and reflects on his or her context and theology. Cutting across denominational, gender, disciplinary, international and generational boundaries to explore shifts in theology and methodology, this book provides a diagnostic tool for examining where theology has come from and a compass to where theology is headed. Contributors include: James H. Cone, Edward Farley, Colin E. Gunton, Alister E. McGrath, Wayne A. Meeks, John Milbank, Jürgen Moltmann, Gerald O'Collins, Rosemary Radford Ruether, Kathryn Tanner, Keith Ward and John Webster.

D0148939

Shaping a Theological Mind

Theological context and methodology

DARREN C. MARKS
Wycliffe Hall and St Hugh's College, Oxford

ASHGATE

Published by
Ashgate Publishing Limited
Gower House
Croft Road
Aldershot
Hants GU11 3HR
England

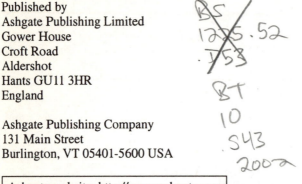

Ashgate Publishing Company
131 Main Street
Burlington, VT 05401-5600 USA

Ashgate website: http://www.ashgate.com

British Library Cataloguing in Publication Data
Shaping a theological mind : theological context and
   methodology
   1. Theology
   I. Marks, Darren C.
   230

Library of Congress Cataloging-in-Publication Data
Shaping a theological mind: theological context and methodology / edited by
   Darren C. Marks.
         p. cm.
      ISBN 0-7546-0616-3 (hbk.)
      ISBN 0-7546-0617-1 (pbk.)
         1. Theology, Doctrinal. I. Marks, Darren C.

   BT10 .S43 2002
   230'.01–dc21

                                                                    2002023645

ISBN 0 7546 0616 3 (Hbk)
ISBN 0 7546 0617 1 (Pbk)

Typeset in Times by J.L. & G.A. Wheatley Design, Aldershot and printed in Great Britain by MPG Books Ltd, Bodmin, Cornwall

Contents

Contributors

James H. Cone, Briggs Distinguished Professor of Theology, Union Theological Seminary.

Edward Farley, Emeritus Buffington Professor of Theology, Vanderbilt University.

Colin E. Gunton, Professor of Christian Doctrine, King's College London.

Alister E. McGrath, Professor of Historical Theology, University of Oxford and Principal of Wycliffe Hall, Oxford.

Wayne A. Meeks, Emeritus Woolsey Professor of Biblical Studies, Yale University.

John Milbank, Francis Ball Professor of Philosophical Theology, University of Virginia.

Jürgen Moltmann, Emeritus Professor of Systematic Theology, University of Tübingen.

Gerald O'Collins SJ, Professor of Theology, Pontifical Gregorian University (Rome).

Rosemary Radford Ruether, Carpenter Professor of Feminist Theology, Graduate Theological Union (Berkeley).

Kathryn Tanner, Professor of Theology, University of Chicago Divinity School.

Keith Ward, Regius Professor of Divinity, University of Oxford.

John Webster, Lady Margaret Professor of Divinity, University of Oxford.

Preface

The genesis of this text is admittedly somewhat selfish. As a youngish would-be theologian, fresh out of graduate studies, and imbued with a sense of wonder at the 'cathedrals of the mind' of many theologians, I wanted to ask questions that reading texts alone would not permit. The most pressing question was the hardest to answer: 'why theology at all?' To ask 'why theology?' was to ask the question of the authors' own lives and contexts, for it is clear from reading the essays that each participant understands constructive theology as a form of *habitus theosdotos* – the concurrence of their own contingent circumstances in a greater culture (and its own problematic questions for theology) with their sense of what the Gospel demands for, to borrow a Barthian term, 'theological existence' today. Or, put more simply and perhaps 'spiritualized', in the confluence of their lives, experiences and education (both formal and informal) with their theological writings, the question of how each is faithful to their sense of call to the Christian faith is explored. In each essay what cannot be denied is the sense that *what* is being said (about faith and theology) reflects a greater *Who* in light of a host of real and concrete issues. This is, not at all, merely the preoccupation with the epistemological justification for theology that contemporary theology is oft charged, but real theological *praxis*. The issues of each's work are the very issues of each individual thinker living within their own sense of grace-vocation and provocation or challenge to Christian solution. Each, as a theologian, is a 'hearer' and 'preacher', their works being 'sermons' of their profession in Christ.

The mandate given to each participant was to reflect on his or her context and theology. However, to distinguish from the notable *How My Mind has Changed* series, the focus was not to be on the alteration within theology (although immutability is a negative quality even for God) but rather on the consistency in development. Many in the volume have used the motif of 'pilgrimage'; this is particularly apropos, in that a pilgrim might encounter many obstacles or adventures in the journey but sets out with a purpose to arrive somewhere specific. In a like manner, each thinker in the volume was asked to consider what purpose their theological journey was to seek, even given radical shifts in the process. A second mandate was to attempt to provide a theological 'state-of-the-union' by cutting across denomination, gender, discipline, location and even status of career. It is the latter categories that yield the most fruit, allowing a comparison between European, British and American theology and also a comparison from very senior thinkers such as Meeks, Moltmann, Ruether, Cone and O'Collins to those in very promising mid- or maturing careers such as Tanner, Milbank, Webster, Farley, Gunton and Ward. Of course, the limited nature of the text, combined with the notable absence of many deserving thinkers, puts limits on this function. It can only be confessed that, despite best intentions, there is a measure of selection in the authors not only by personal preference but by factors such as health and time constraints. As such, some hoped for, particularly some French theologians, could not participate.

This work is dedicated to my own teachers, in theology and in life. From Professor Webster and Professor McGrath I have learnt not only the skills, such as I have, of a scholar but, more importantly, the skill of being a Christian person in my vocation. From my father, Gary Marks, I have learnt how to be a father and a good man. These skills, for that is what they are, I hope to pass on to my own son, Gareth Arturo, who has shown me in two years the urgency of all the previous lessons. Finally, I thank each contributor of the volume for teaching me that theology is a passionate discipline, that it matters and that it serves.

D.C. Marks
Oxford

Chapter 1

Looking Back, Going Forward

James H. Cone

When I think about my vocation, I go back to my childhood years in Bearden, Arkansas, a rural community of approximately 1200 people. I do not remember Bearden for nostalgic reasons. In fact, I seldom return there in person, because of persistent racial tension in my relations with the whites and lingering ambivalence in my feelings towards the blacks. I am not and do not wish to be Bearden's favourite son. My brother, Cecil, also a theologian and preacher, has been bestowed that honour by the African–American community, a distinction he gladly accepts and a role he fulfils quite well.

I remember Bearden because it is the place where I first discovered myself – as *black* and *Christian*. There, the meaning of *black* was defined primarily by the menacing presence of whites, which no African–American could escape. I grew up during the age of Jim Crow (1940s and early 1950s). I attended segregated schools, drank water from 'coloured' fountains, went to movies in balconies, and when absolutely necessary greeted white adults at the back door of their homes. I also observed the contempt and brutality that white law meted out to the blacks who transgressed their racial *mores* or who dared to question their authority. Bearden white people, like most southerners of that time, could be mean and vicious, and I, along with other blacks, avoided them whenever possible as if they were poisonous snakes.

The Christian part of my identity was shaped primarily at Macedonia African Methodist Episcopal (AME) Church. Every Sunday and sometimes on weeknights, I encountered Jesus through rousing sermons, fervent prayers, spirited gospel songs and the passionate testimonies of the people. Jesus was the dominant reality at Macedonia and in black life in Bearden. The people walked with him and told him about their troubles as if he were a trusted friend who understood their trials and tribulations in this unfriendly world. They called Jesus 'the lily of the valley and the bright and morning star', the 'Rose of Sharon and the Lord of life' and a 'very present help in time of trouble'. The people often shouted and danced, clapped their hands and stamped their feet as they bore witness to the power of Jesus' Spirit in their midst, 'building them up where they are torn down and propping them up on every leaning side'.

Like the people of Macedonia, Jesus became a significant presence in my life too. I do not remember the exact date or time I 'turned to Jesus', as the conversion experience was called. At home, church and school, at play and at

1

work, Jesus was always there, as the anchor of life, giving it meaning and purpose and bestowing hope and faith in the ultimate justice of things. Jesus was that reality who empowered black people to know that they were not the worthless human beings that white people said they were.

There were no atheists in 'Cotton Belt', as the 'coloured' section of Bearden was called – no proclaimers of Nietzsche's 'God is dead' philosophy and none of the 'cultured despisers' of religion that Schleiermacher wrote to in 1799. The closest to Nietzsche's atheists and Schleiermacher's 'cultured despisers' were the bluespeople who drank corn whiskey and slowly and sensually boogied to the deep guttural sound of the raunchy music at the 'jook' joints every Friday and Saturday night. The sounds of Bessie Smith, Muddy Waters and Howlin' Wolf took centre stage as they belted out 'I Used To Be Your Sweet Mama', 'Hoochie Coochie Man' and 'Somebody in My Home'. Such music was called the 'lowdown dirty blues'.

Unlike the churchpeople, the bluespeople found the Sunday religion of Jesus inadequate for coping with their personal problems and the social contradictions they experienced during the week. As church people soothed their souls with the song 'Lord, I Want to Be a Christian in My Heart', the people at the honky-tonk transcended their agony by facing it with stoic defiance or, as James Baldwin called it, 'ironic tenacity':[1] 'I got the blues but I'm too damned mean to cry.'

Sometimes sharp tensions emerged between the celebrants of Saturday night and those of Sunday morning. But each group respected the other, because both knew that they were seeking, in their own way, to cope with the same troubles of life. Some people moved between the two groups during different periods of their lives, as my father did. But it was not possible to be a member in good standing in both groups at the same time, because the church demanded that an individual make a choice between the blues and the spirituals, between the 'devil's music' and the 'sweet melodies of Jesus'. Baptist and Methodist churches, the only black denominations in Bearden, regularly accepted backsliders back into the fold, provided they repented of their wrongdoing and declared their intentions to lead a good and righteous life in service to the Lord. My father had a few lapses in faith, because he found it hard to cope with life's adversities without taking a nip of gin and hanging out with the bluespeople in order to add a little spice to life not found at the church. But my mother monitored him closely, and Macedonia readily received him back into the community of the faithful as often as he publicly repented.

What puzzled me most during my childhood about the religion of Jesus was not the tension between Saturday night and Sunday morning in black life but rather the conspicuous presence of the colour bar in white churches. In Bearden, like the rest of America, Sunday was the most segregated day of the week, and 11:00 am the most segregated hour. Black and white Christians had virtually no social or religious dealings with each other, even though both were Baptists and Methodists – reading the same Bible, worshipping the same God, and reciting the same confessions of faith in their congregations.

Although whites posted 'Welcome' signs outside their churches ostensibly beckoning all visitors to join them in worship, blacks knew that the invitation did not include them. 'What kind of Christianity is it that preaches love and practises segregation?', my brother Cecil and I, budding young theologians, often asked each other. 'How could whites exclude black people from their churches and still claim Jesus as their Saviour and the Bible as their holy book?' We talked about testing the theological integrity of white faith by seeking to integrate one of their churches, but felt that the risks of bodily harm were too great.

Despite the ever-present reality of white supremacy, I do not ever remember experiencing a feeling of inferiority because of what whites said about me or about other black people. One reason was the stellar example my father and mother set before me. They were part of that cloud of black witnesses that James Baldwin wrote about who, 'in the teeth of the most terrible odds, achieved an unassailable and monumental dignity'.[2] They taught me what Baldwin told his nephew: 'You can only be destroyed by believing that you really are what the white world calls a *nigger*.'[3]

My parents were strong and self-confident, exhibiting a determined opposition to white supremacy and creative leadership and great courage when they and the black community faced adversity. Charlie and Lucy, as the black people in Bearden affectionately called them, were immensely intelligent, even though they had little opportunity for formal education, having completed only the sixth and ninth grades, respectively. (With the support and encouragement of my father, my mother went back and completed the high school where her sons had graduated earlier and also went on to finish her college degree four years later. She then returned to teach in Bearden. I was struck by her determination.) Their education, they often told their sons, came from the 'school of hard knocks' – the experience of surviving with dignity in a society that did not recognize black humanity.

The faith of Macedonia, which my parents imbibed deeply, was a powerful antidote against the belief that blacks were less than whites. According to *this* faith, God created all people equal – as brothers and sisters in the church and the society. No person or group is better than any other. As evidence for that claim, preachers and teachers often cited the text from the prophet Malachi: 'Have we not all one father? hath not one God created us?' (Malachi 2:10 KJV). They also quoted Paul, *selectively* – carefully avoiding the ambiguous and problematic texts, especially where Paul returned the slave Onesimus to his master (Philemon 1:12) and where servants were told to 'be obedient to them that are *your* masters ... as unto Christ' (Ephesians 6:5 KJV).

Preachers and Sunday School teachers at Macedonia were quite skilled in picking biblical texts that affirmed their humanity. They especially liked Luke's account of Paul's sermon on Mars' Hill where he said God 'made of one blood all nations of men [and women] for to dwell on all the face of the Earth ...' (Acts 17:26 KJV). They also quoted Paul's letter to the Galatians: 'There is neither Jew nor Greek ... neither bond nor free ... neither male nor female' (Galatians 3:28 KJV). We are 'all one in Christ Jesus' – blacks and whites, as well as other human colours, genders and orientations. When one truly believes that gospel and internalizes it in one's way of life, as I and many black Christians in Bearden did, it is possible to know that 'you are somebody', even though the world treats you like nobody.

From the time I was conscious of being black and Christian, I recognized that I was a problem for America's white politicians and invisible to most of its practitioners of religion. I did not quite understand what made me a problem or invisible since skin colour appeared to be a minor difference between human beings. Yet politicians found it difficult to pass laws to protect black humanity. Even those that were passed were rarely enforced. White ministers seemed not to notice the daily white assault on black humanity. They preached sermons about loving God and neighbour as if the violence that whites committed against blacks did not invalidate their Christian identity.

While struggling to understand how whites reconciled racism with their Christian identity, I also encountered an uncritical faith in many black churches. They not only seemed to tolerate anti-intellectualism as whites tolerated racism, but they, like most whites in relation to racism, often promoted it. It was as if the less one knew and the louder one shouted Jesus' name, the closer one was to God.

I found it hard to believe that the God of Jesus condoned ignorance as if it was a virtue. It contradicted what my parents and teachers taught me about the value of education and a disciplined mind. It also contradicted what I read in history books about black slaves who risked life and limb in order to learn to read and write so they could understand more clearly the meaning of the freedom to which God had called them. I was, therefore, deeply troubled by the anti-intellectualism that permeated many aspects of the ministry in the black church.

How could ministers preach the gospel in a world they did not understand? How could they understand the Gospel without disciplined reflections and critical debate? 'A religion that won't stand the application of reason and common sense,' wrote W.E.B. Du Bois, 'is not fit for an intelligent dog.'[4]

The search for a reasoned faith in a complex and ever-changing world was the chief motivation that led me to study at Garrett Theological Seminary (now Garrett-Evangelical). It seemed that the more I learned about the Gospel through a critical study of the Bible, history, theology and the practice of ministry, the more I needed and wanted to know about it. I wanted to explore its meanings for different social, political and cultural contexts, past and present.

Theology quickly became my favourite subject in seminary because it opened the door to explore faith's meaning for the current time and situation in which I was living. I loved the give and take of theological debate and eagerly waited for the opportunity during and after classes to engage my professors and fellow students on the burning theological issues of the day. That was why I remained at Garrett and Northwestern University for the PhD in systematic theology. After I completed the doctorate in the spring of 1965, writing a dissertation on Karl Barth's anthropology, I thought I had enough knowledge of the Christian faith to communicate it to people anywhere in the world. Who would not feel adequately endowed after reading twelve volumes of Barth's *Church Dogmatics*?

But the Civil Rights and Black Power movements of the 1960s awakened me from my theological slumber. As I became actively involved in the Black Freedom movement that was exploding in the streets all over America, I soon discovered how limited my seminary education had been. The curriculum at Garrett and Northwestern had not dealt with questions that black people were asking as they searched for the theological meaning of their fight for justice in a white racist society. And as individuals and isolated students within a demanding educational system, neither I nor the other token number of black students had the intellectual resources to articulate them. I found myself grossly ill-prepared, because I knew deep down that I could not repeat to a struggling black community the doctrines of the faith as they had been reinterpreted by Barth, Bultmann, Niebuhr and Tillich for European colonizers and white racists in the United States. I knew that, before I could say anything worthwhile about God and the black situation of oppression in the USA, I had to discover a theological identity that was accountable to the life, history and culture of African–American people.

In a way, my education had pulled me away from my people. The educational quest had been to master the theological systems of mostly well-known European theologians of the past and present. As students, we obediently spent most of our time reading books, listening to lectures and writing papers about their views of God, Jesus, the Holy Spirit and the church. But recognizing the community to whom I was accountable, I wanted to know more than just what Europeans and white Americans who emulated them thought about sacred reality. I was searching for a way to create a Christian theology out of the black experience of slavery, segregation and the struggle for a just society. When I asked my professors about what theology had to do with the black struggle for racial justice, they seemed surprised and uncomfortable with the question, not knowing what to say, and anxious to move on with the subject matter as they understood it. I was often told that theology and the struggle for racial justice were separate subjects, with the latter belonging properly in the disciplines of sociology and political science. Although I felt a disquieting unease with that response, I did not say much about it to my professors as they skirted around talking about what the Gospel had to say to black people in a white society that had defined them as non-persons.

While reading Martin Luther King Jr and Malcolm X, the blackness in my theological consciousness exploded like a volcano after many dormant years. I found my theological voice. Using the cultural and political insights of Malcolm and Martin, I discovered a way of articulating what I wanted to say about theology and race that not only rejected the need for my professors' approval, but challenged them to exorcise the racism in their theologies.

Malcolm taught me how to make theology black and never again to despise my African origin. Martin showed me how to make and keep theology Christian and never allow it to be used to support injustice. I was transformed from a *negro* theologian to a *black* theologian, from an understanding of theology as an analysis of God-ideas in books to an understanding of it as a disciplined reflection about God arising out of a commitment to the practice of justice for the poor.

The turn to blackness was an even deeper *metanoia* experience than the previous turn to Jesus. It was truly spiritual, transforming radically my way of seeing the world and doing theology. Before I was born again into thinking black, I thought of theology as something remote from my history and culture, something that was primarily defined by Europeans and which I, at best, could only imitate. Blackness gave me new theological spectacles, which enabled me to move beyond the limits of white theology, and empowered my mind to think wild, heretical thoughts when evaluated by white academic values. Blackness opened my eyes to see African–American history and culture as one of the most insightful sources for knowing about God since the Bible was declared a canon. Blackness whetted my appetite for learning how to do theology with a black signature on it and thereby make it accountable to poor black people and not to the privileged white theological establishment. The revolution that Malcolm X created in my theological consciousness meant that I could no longer make peace with the intellectual mediocrity in which I had been trained. The more I trusted my experience, the more new thoughts about God and theology whirled around in my head – so fast I could hardly contain my excitement.

Using the black experience as the starting point of theology raised the theodicy question in a profound and challenging way that was never mentioned in graduate school. It was James Baldwin's *Fire Next Time* that poignantly defined the problem for me: 'If [God's] love was so great, and if He loved all His children, why were we, the blacks, cast down so far?'[5] This was an existential, heart-wrenching question, which challenged the academic way in which the problem of evil was dealt with in graduate school. It forced me to search deep into a wellspring of blackness, not for a theoretical answer that would satisfy the dominant intellectual culture of Europe and the USA, but rather for a new way of doing theology that would empower the suffering black poor to fight for a more liberated existence.

In writing *Black Theology and Black Power* (1969), I suddenly understood what Karl Barth must have felt when he first rejected the liberal theology of his professors in Germany. It was a liberating experience to be free of my liberal and neo-orthodox professors, to be liberated from defining theology with abstract theological jargon that was unrelated to the life-and-death issues of black people. Although separated by nearly 50 years and dealing with completely different theological situations and issues, I felt a spiritual kinship with Barth, especially his writing of *The Epistle to the Romans* (1921) and in his public debate with Adolf von Harnack, his former teacher.

As I think back to that time in the late 1960s, when white American theologians were writing and talking about the 'Death of God theology' as black people were fighting and dying in the streets, my energy swells once again. I was angry and could not keep it to myself. Like Malcolm X, I felt I was the angriest black theologian in America.[6] I had to speak out, as forcefully as I knew how, against the racism I witnessed in theology, the churches and the broader society. And that was why I began to write.

The anger I felt while writing *Black Theology and Black Power* was fuelled by the assassination of Martin Luther King Jr. More than 30 years later, I am still just as angry, because America, when viewed from the perspective of the black poor, is no closer to King's dream of a just society than when he was killed. While the black middle class has made considerable economic progress, the underclass, despite America's robust economy, is worse off in 2001 than in 1968. Although the statistics are well known, they still fail to shock or outrage most Americans. One-third of young black males are involved in the criminal justice system. One-half of black babies are born in poverty, and their life expectancy in the urban ghetto is lower than that of Bangladesh.

America is still two societies: one rich and middle class and the other poor and working class. One-third of the African–American population is poor. Predominantly women and children, they are, in the words of William J. Wilson, 'the truly disadvantaged',[7] with few skills that enable them to compete in this technological, informational age. To recognize the plight of the poor does not require academic dissection. It requires only a drive into the central cities of the nation to see people living in places not fit for human habitation.

What deepens my anger today is the appalling silence of white theologians on racism in the USA and the modern world. Whereas this silence has been partly broken in several secular disciplines, theology remains virtually mute. From Walter Rauschenbusch and Reinhold Niebuhr up to the present moment, progressive white theologians, with few exceptions, write and teach as if they do not need to address the radical contradiction that racism creates for Christian theology. They do not write about slavery, colonialism, segregation and the profound cultural link these horrible crimes created between white supremacy and Christianity. The cultural bond between European values and Christian beliefs is so deeply woven in the American psyche and thought process that their identification is assumed. White images and ideas dominate the religious life of Christians and the intellectual life of theologians, reinforcing the 'moral' right of white people to dominate people of colour economically and politically. White supremacy is so widespread that it becomes a 'natural' way of viewing the world. We must ask therefore: is racism so deeply embedded in Euro-American history and culture that it is impossible to do theology without being anti-black?

There is historical precedent for such ideological questioning. After the Jewish Holocaust, Christian theologians were forced to ask whether anti-Judaism was so deeply woven into the core of the Gospel and Western history that theology was no longer possible without being anti-Semitic. Recently, feminists asked an equally radical question regarding whether patriarchy was so deeply rooted in biblical faith and its male theological tradition that one could not do Christian theology without justifying the oppression of women. Gay and lesbian theologians are following the feminist lead and are asking whether homophobia is an inherent part of biblical faith. And finally, Third World theologians, particularly in Latin America, forced many progressive First World theologians to revisit Marx's class critique of religion or run the risk of making Christianity a tool for exploiting the poor.

Race criticism is just as crucial for the integrity of Christian theology as any critique in the modern world. Christianity was blatantly used to justify slavery, colonialism and segregation for nearly 500 years. And yet this great contradiction has been and is consistently neglected by the same white male theologians, who seemingly never ignore the problem that critical reason poses for faith in a secular world. They still do theology as if white supremacy creates no serious problem for Christian belief. Their silence on race is so conspicuous that I sometimes wonder why they are not greatly embarrassed by it.

How do we account for such a long history of white theological blindness to racism and its brutal impact on the lives of African people? Is it because white theologians do not know about the tortured history of the Atlantic slave trade, which, according to British historian Basil Davidson, 'cost Africa at least fifty million souls?'[8] Have they forgotten about the unspeakable crimes of colonialism? In the Congo alone, 'reputable estimates suggest that between 5 and 8 million [people] were killed in the course of twenty-three years'.[9]

Two hundred and forty-four years of slavery and 100 years of legal segregation, augmented by a reign of white terror that lynched more than 5000 blacks, defined the meaning of America as 'white over black'.[10] White supremacy shaped the social, political, economic, cultural and religious ethos in the churches, the academy and the broader society. Seminary and divinity school professors contributed to America's white nationalist perspective by openly advocating the superiority of the white race over all others. The highly-regarded church historian, Philip Schaff of Union Seminary in New York (1870–93) spoke for most white theologians in the nineteenth century when he said: 'The Anglo-Saxon and Anglo-American, of all modern races, possess the strongest national character and the one best fitted for universal dominion.'[11]

Present-day white theologians do not express their racist views as blatantly as Philip Schaff. They do not even speak of the 'negro's cultural backwardness', as America's best-known social ethicist Reinhold Niebuhr often did, and as late as 1965.[12] To speak as Schaff and Niebuhr spoke would be politically incorrect in this era of 'multiculturalism' and 'colour blindness', but that does not mean that today's white theologians are less racist. It only means that their racism is concealed or unconscious. As long as religion scholars do not engage racism in their intellectual work, we can be sure that they are as racist as their grandparents, whether they know it or not. By not engaging America's crimes against black people, white theologians are treating the nation's violent racist past as if it is dead. But as William Faulkner said, 'the past is never dead; it is not even past'. Racism is so deeply embedded in American history and culture that we cannot get rid of this cancer by simply ignoring it.

There can be no justice without memory – without remembering the horrible crimes committed against humanity and the great human struggles for justice. But oppressors always try to erase the history of their crimes and often portray themselves as the innocent ones. Through their control of the media, as well as their control of the religious, political and academic discourse, 'they're able,' as Malcolm put it, 'to make the victim look like the criminal and the criminal look like the victim'.[13]

Even when white theologians reflect on God and suffering – that is, the problem of theodicy – they almost never make racism a central issue in their analysis of the challenge that evil poses for the Christian faith. If they should happen to mention racism, it is usually just a footnote or only a marginal comment. They almost never make racism the subject of a sustained analysis. It is amazing that racism could be so prevalent and violent in American life and yet so absent in white theological discourse.

During his presidency, Bill Clinton called for a national dialogue on race and created a context for public debate in the churches, the academy and the broader society. Where were the white theologians? What guidance did they provide for this debate? Did they create a theological understanding of racism that enabled whites to have a meaningful conversation with blacks and other people of colour? Unfortunately, instead of searching for an understanding of the great racial divide, white religion scholars are doing their searching in the form of a third quest for the historical Jesus. I am not opposed to this academic quest. But if we could get a significant number of white theologians to study racism as seriously as they investigate the historical Jesus and other academic topics, they might discover how deep the cancer of racism is embedded not only in the society but also in the narrow way in which the discipline of theology is understood.

Although black liberation theology emerged out of the Civil Rights and Black Power movements in the 1960s, white theologians ignored it as if it was not worthy to be engaged as an academic discipline. It was not until Orbis Books published the translated works of Latin American liberation theologians that white North American male theologians cautiously began to talk and write about liberation theology and God's solidarity with the poor. But they still ignored the black poor in the USA, Africa, Asia and Latin America. Our struggle to make sense out of the fight for racial justice was dismissed as too narrow and divisive. White American theologians used the Latin American focus on *class* in order to minimize and even dismiss the black focus on *race*. African–Americans wondered how American whites could take sides with the poor 'out there' in Latin America without first siding with the poor 'here' in North America. It was as if they had forgotten about their own complicity in the suffering of the black poor who were often only a stone's throw from the seminaries and universities in which they taught theology.

White theology's amnesia about racism is partly due to the failure of black theologians to mount a persistently radical race critique of Christian theology, one so incisive and enduring that no one could do theology without engaging white supremacy in the modern world. American and European theologians became concerned about anti-Semitism only because Jews did not let them forget the Christian complicity in the Holocaust. Feminists transformed the consciousness of American theologians through persistent, hard-hitting analysis of the evils of patriarchy, refusing to let any man anywhere in the world forget the past and present male assault against women. It is always the grassroots intellectuals of an exploited group who must take the lead in exposing the hidden crimes of criminals.

Although black theologians' initial attack on white religion shocked white theologians, we did not shake the racist foundation of modern white theology.[14] With the assistance of James Forman's 'Black Manifesto'[15] and the black caucuses in Protestant denominations, black theological critiques of racism were successful in shaking up the white *churches*. But white theologians in the seminaries, university departments of religion and divinity schools, and professional societies refused to acknowledge racism as a *theological* problem and continued their business as usual, as if the lived experience of blacks was theologically irrelevant.

One reason why black theologians have not developed an enduring radical race critique stems from our uncritical identification with the dominant Christian and integrationist tradition in African–American history. We are the children of the Black Church and the Civil Rights Movement. The spirituals have informed our theology more than the blues, Howard Thurman more than W.E.B. Du Bois, Martin Luther King Jr more than Malcolm X, and male preachers more than women writers. We failed to sustain the critical side of the black theological dialectic and opted for acceptance into white Christian America. When whites opened the door to receive a token number of us into the academy, church and society, the radical edge of our race critique was quickly dropped as we enjoyed our newfound privileges.

Womanist and second-generation black male theologians, biblical scholars and historians are moving in the right directions. The strength of these new intellectual developments lies in their refusal simply to repeat the ideas of the original advocates of black theology. They are breaking new theological ground, building on, challenging and moving beyond the founders of black theology. Using the writings of Zora Neale Hurston, Alice Walker, Toni Morrison and a host of other women writers past and present, womanist theologians broke the monopoly of black male theological discourse. They challenged the male advocates of black theology to broaden their narrow focus on race and liberation and to incorporate gender, class and sexuality critiques and the themes of survival and quality of life in our theological discourse.[16] Some younger black male critics locate the limits of black theology in its focus on blackness,[17] and others urge a deeper commitment to it, focusing especially on the slave narratives.[18] Still others suggest that the Christian identity of black theology contributes to black passivity in the face of suffering.[19] Biblical scholars and historians are laying exegetical and historical foundations for a critical re-reading of the Bible in the light of the history and culture of black people.[20] All these critiques and proposals make important contributions to the future development of black theology. But what troubles me about all these new theological constructs is the absence of a truly radical race critique.

Malcolm X was the most formidable race critic in the USA during the twentieth century. He was the great master of suspicion in regard to American democracy and the Christian faith. His critique of racism in Christianity and American culture was so forceful that even black Christians were greatly disturbed when they heard his radical analysis. His contention that 'Christianity was a white man's religion' was so persuasive that many black Christians left churches to join the Nation of Islam. The rapid growth of the religion of Islam in the African–American community is largely due to the effectiveness of Malcolm's portrayal of Christianity as white nationalism. It was Malcolm via the Black Power Movement who forced black theologians to take a critical look at white religion and to develop a 'hermeneutic of suspicion' regarding black Christianity. How can African–Americans merge the 'double self' – the black and the Christian – 'into a better and truer self',[21] especially since Africa is the object of ridicule in the modern world and Christianity is hardly distinguishable from European culture?

Although we black theologians appropriated Malcolm in our initial critique of white religion, we did not wrestle with Malcolm long enough. We quickly turned to Martin King. Our mistake was not in moving towards King but rather in leaving Malcolm behind. We need them both as a double-edged sword to slay the dragon of theological racism. Martin and Malcolm represent the *yin* and *yang* in the black attack on racism. One without the other misses the target: the affirmation of blackness in the beloved community of humankind.

Malcolm X teaches us that African–Americans cannot be free without accepting their blackness, without loving Africa as the place of their origin and meaning. Martin King teaches us that no people can be free except in the beloved community of humankind – not just blacks with blacks or whites with whites but all of us together (including Native Americans, Asian/Pacific Islanders, Hispanics, gays, lesbians, bisexuals and transsexuals) in a truly multicultural community. Malcolm alone makes it too easy for blacks to go it alone and for whites to say 'begone!' Martin alone makes it too easy for whites to ask for reconciliation without justice and for middle-class blacks to grant it, as long as they are treated as special. Putting Martin and Malcolm together enables us to overcome the limitations of each and to build on the strengths of both and thereby move people of colour and whites towards racial healing and understanding.

There can be no racial healing without dialogue, without ending the white silence on racism. There can be no reconciliation without honest and frank conversation. Racism is still with us in the academy, in the churches and in every segment of society because we would rather push this problem under the rug than find a way to deal with its past and present manifestations.

Most whites do not like to talk about racism because it makes them feel guilty, a truly uncomfortable feeling. They would rather forget about the past and think only about the present and future. I understand that. But I only ask whites to consider how uncomfortable the victims of racism must feel, as they try to cope with the attitudes of whites acting as if racism ceased with the passage of the 1964 Civil Rights Act. At least when people express their racism overtly, there is some public recognition of its existence and a possibility of racial healing. Silence is racism's best friend.

'A time comes when silence is betrayal,'[22] Martin King said. That time has come for white theologians. Racism is one of the great contradictions of the Gospel in modern times. White theologians who do not oppose racism publicly, and rigorously engage it in their writings, are a part of the problem and must be exposed as the enemy of justice. No one, therefore, can be neutral or silent in the face of this great evil. We are either for or against it.

Black theologians must end their silence too. We have opposed racism much too gently. We have permitted white theological silence in exchange for the rewards of being accepted by the white theological establishment. This is a terrible price to pay for the few crumbs that drop from the white master's table. We must replace theological deference with courage, and thereby confront, openly and lovingly, silent white racists or be condemned as participants in the betrayal of our own people.

In 1903, W.E.B. Du Bois prophesied, 'The problem of the twentieth century is the problem of the color-line, the relation of the darker to the lighter races of [people] in Asia and Africa, in America and the islands of the sea.'[23] As we stand at the beginning of the twenty-first century, that remarkable prophecy is as relevant today as it was when Du Bois uttered it. The challenge for black theology in this century is to develop an enduring race critique that is so comprehensively woven into Christian understanding that no one will be able to forget the horrible crimes of white supremacy in the modern world.

Notes

1   James Baldwin (1964), *Fire Next Time*, New York: Dell, p.61.
2   Baldwin, p.21.
3   Baldwin, p.14.
4   Manning Marable (1985), 'The Black Faith of W.E.B. Du Bois: Sociocultural and Political Dimensions of Black Religion', *The Southern Quarterly*, v. xxiii, no. 3, p.21.
5   Baldwin, p.46.
6   Many people called Malcolm X 'the angriest Negro in America'. See Malcolm X with Alex Haley (1965; reprint 1986), *Autobiography*, New York: Ballantine Books, p.366.
7   William Julius Wilson (1987), *The Truly Disadvantaged: The Inner City, the Underclass and Public Policy*, Chicago: University of Chicago Press.
8   Basil Davidson (1961), *The African Slave Trade: Precolonial History 1450–1850*, Boston: Little, Brown and Co., p.80.

9   Louis Turner (1973), *Multinational Companies and the Third World*, New York: Hill and Wang, p.27.

10 See especially Winthrop D. Jordan (1969), *White Over Black: American Attitudes Toward the Negro 1550–1812*, Baltimore: Penguin Books.

11 Martin E. Marty (1970), *Righteous Empire: The Protestant Experience in America*, New York: Dial Press, p.17.

12 Reinhold Niebuhr (1965), 'Man's Tribalism As One Source of His Inhumanity', in *Man's Nature and His Communities*, New York: Scribner; and (1958), 'Justice to the American Negro from State, Community and Church', in *Pious and Secular America*, New York: Scribner.

13 Malcolm X (1965), *Malcolm X Speaks*, New York: Grove Press, p.165.

14 In addition to *Black Theology and Black Power*, my contribution to black theology's race critique included *A Black Theology of Liberation* (1970, 1985) and *God of the Oppressed* (1975, 1998). Other critiques were Albert B. Cleage (1968), *The Black Messiah*, New York: Sheed; J. Deotis Roberts (1971, 1994), *Liberation and Reconciliation: A Black Theology*, Maryknoll, NY: Orbis; (1974), *A Black Political Theology*, Philadelphia: Westminster; and Gayraud S. Wilmore (1972, 1998), *Black Religion and Black Radicalism*, Maryknoll, NY: Orbis. Significant essays included Vincent Harding (1967), 'Black Power and the American Christ', *Christian Century*, 4; (1968), 'The Religion of Black Power', in D.R. Cutler (ed.), *Religious Situation*, Boston: Beacon.

15 See 'The Black Manifesto', in James H. Cone and Gayraud S. Wilmore (eds) (1993), *Black Theology: A Documentary History, Vol. One, 1966–79*, Maryknoll, NY: Orbis.

16 See 'Womanist Theology', in James H. Cone and Gayraud S. Wilmore (eds) (1993), *Black Theology: A Documentary History, Vol. Two, 1980–1992*, Maryknoll, NY: Orbis.

17 See Victor Anderson (1995), *Beyond Ontological Blackness: An Essay on African–American Religious and Cultural Criticism*, New York: Continuum.

18 See 'The Second Generation', in Cone and Wilmore (eds), *Black Theology: A Documentary History, Vol. Two, 1980–1992*, pp.15–75; see also Josiah U. Young (1992), *A Pan-African Theology: Providence and the Legacies of the Ancestors*, Trenton, NJ: Africa World Press; Dwight N. Hopkins and George Cummings (1991), *Cut Loose Your Stammering Tongue: Black Theology in the Slave Narratives*, Maryknoll, NY: Orbis; Dwight N. Hopkins (1993), *Shoes That Fit Our Feet: Sources for a Constructive Black Theology*, Maryknoll, NY: Orbis; Garth Kasimu Baker-Fletcher (1996), *Xodus: An African–American Male Journey*, Minneapolis: Fortress; and Riggins R. Earl (1993), *Dark Symbols, Obscure Signs: God, Self, and Community in the Slave Mind*, Maryknoll, NY: Orbis.

19 Anthony B. Pinn (1995), *Why, Lord? Suffering and Evil in Black Theology*, New York: Continuum. Pinn is building on an earlier critique of black theology by William R. Jones (1973, 1998), *Is God A White Racist? A Preamble to Black Theology*, Boston: Beacon.

20 See 'New Directions in Black Biblical Interpretation', in Cone and Wilmore (eds), *Black Theology: A Documentary History, Vol. Two, 1980–1992*, pp.177–254; Cain H. Felder (1989), *Troubling Biblical Waters: Race, Class, and Family*, Maryknoll, NY: Orbis; (1991), *Stony the Road We Trod: African–American Biblical Interpretation*, Minneapolis: Fortress; Brian K. Blount (1998), *Go Preach! Mark's Kingdom Message and the Black Church Today*, Maryknoll, NY: Orbis; and T.H. Smith (1994), *Conjuring Culture: Biblical Formations of Black America*, New York: Oxford University Press.

21 W.E.B. Du Bois (1961), *The Souls of Black Folk*, Greenwich, Conn.: Facett, p.23.

22 Martin Luther King Jr (1967), 'Beyond Vietnam', a pamphlet of the Clergy and Laymen Concerned About Vietnam.

23 Du Bois, p.23.

Chapter 2

Ecclesial Contextual Thinking

Edward Farley

The Meaning of Context

To say that constructive theology is contextual is both self-evident and, to a certain degree, imprecise. That theology (and the theologian) is subject to cultural influences goes without saying. What human undertaking, or for that matter any finite entity, escapes influence? But what precisely is a context? A definition is ready at hand. Context names the ways in which human life and action are subject to the pushes and pulls of an environment. But 'environment' itself can mean different things: background, situation or location. *Background* names the cosmic, biological and historical conditions of human situations and locations, the 'worlds' and spheres of nature and history. *Situation* names the particular configuration of the elements of background as they bear on an individual, community or other social entity in a particular time and place. A black teenage urbanite lives in a particular situation; a wealthy, gated-community retiree another. Insofar as it pertains to individuals, a situation is biographically and personally centred. Insofar as individuals live together in families, neighbourhoods or ethnic subcultures, they share common situations. Situations are never separated from background, but they differ from background in that the events or elements of situations impinge on and specifically shape the everyday life of individuals or groups. To some degree, human beings are aware of and respond to their situation. If a virus, for instance HIV, spreads from one part of the biosphere to a human group, it becomes part of that group's situation. *Location* names those aspects of a situation that bring about social and psychological identity: gender, class, ethnicity, race, age and subculture.

Any one of these three spheres of influence can determine the meaning of 'context' and 'contextual'. For some thinkers, to be contextual is to hearken to the resources and imperilments of their social identity, their gender for instance. For others, preoccupied with questions of theology and science, 'context' can be as broad as the origin and operations of the cosmos. For yet others, context is as specific as the issues of a local political election.

To say that constructive theology has a 'method' (which relates to context) is likewise imprecise. At one time I was absorbed by questions of method, possibly for good reasons. Once I faced the rather daunting task of theological thinking, once I crossed the line from the relative safety and clarity of

15

interpreting what others had said, I was quite puzzled about how to proceed. 'Method' seemed to promise an answer. Method would help me unearth the buried treasure of theological truth. I soon found out that with method (methodology) came a new set of obscurities. In its most formal sense, method can mean whatever way an inquirer decides to approach a subject matter. But in academic circles, it tends to be linked to descriptive and empirical scholarship. In other words, method connotes science both in the sociological sense of a corporate cognitive endeavour with a distinctive 'institutionality' that includes a special argot, journals, satellite disciplines and professional organizations, and funded research, and in the sense of a clear, public and linear procedure of inquiry and demonstration. Under the sway of this paradigm, I searched out scientific equivalents (or at least parallels) in theology: precise delineation of field (for instance, organic chemistry), subject matter, procedures of inquiry and modes of verification.

Theology, as we know, names a broad and multifaceted phenomenon and many of these characteristics appropriately apply. Yet the more I became preoccupied with what might be called the truth and reality of faith matters, the more the paradigm of science gave way to a paradigm of reflection or, simply, thinking. One issue that pressed me in this direction was the realization that theology was not simply a professional activity done by a clerical or academic elite. Lay persons, believers, even non-believers are quite capable of theological thinking, however limited be their exposure to the rigours of scholarship and however unsophisticated they may be about method. Whether it is taken up by laypersons or career academics, theology as a constructive, truth-oriented endeavour is a thinking. An older time might say 'reasoning', but thinking involves much more than reasoning: clarifying, analysing, uncovering, distinguishing, interrelating, demythologizing, critically exposing, and so on. As there are many types of (constructive) theology, so there are many types of theological thinking, some linear and oriented to logical demonstration, some focused on linguistic clarification, some engaged in phenomenological uncovering or display. A theological school or movement, for instance process theology or confessional theology, typically displays a specific way of thinking. Furthermore, the project of an individual theologian will typically employ more than one type of thinking.

When context becomes part of a thinking or an agenda for thought, it takes on a new meaning. It is one thing to say that any and all of human life is contextual (influenced). It is quite another to say that thinking, a truth-oriented, reflective inquiry, is contextual. Such thinking is of course influenced, that is, specifically shaped by gender and ethnic locations and by the configurations of a situation. But a thinker never thinks everything at once. Even after great effort, human beings are able to identify only a small fraction of the influences that bear on them. Thinkers, thus, are never able to think from or towards the totality of their contexts. Thinking is always selective, programmatic and governed by specific aims. Accordingly, context enters thinking (reflection, criticism, deconstruction, uncovering of meaning, and so on) by way of the aims and agendas of thinking and therefore as something selected, focused on and privileged. For example, being a woman or a man will inevitably shape thinking in a certain way. Being a woman or a man may or may not be explicitly attended in a project of thinking. Thus in a programme of thinking, context takes on the additional connotation of those strands of background, situation and location that are attended to, given thematic and criteriological weight.

Connecting context and thinking has a second outcome. The different facets of context (background, situation and location) evoke or require different ways of thinking. These ways presuppose and draw upon the contexts (influences) already present in the situation and location. The long history of persecution and disenfranchisement of the women of a certain minority group will have already shaped the behaviour, emotional life and cognitive orientations of the women of that group. When a woman of that group takes up the project of (theological) thinking, and directs that thinking from and towards location, a specific kind of thinking will ensue, both from her already shaped orientations and from the way her selected location sets its own requirements. If she thinks from and towards another context, for instance, the relation between economics, political power and justice, her thinking will take on a new embodiment. To summarize, contexts name both a range of influences and, in thinking, selected and weighted themes and problematics taken from that range.

The Meaning of Context for the Faith Community

Something of crucial importance is clearly missing in this exploration of the way context enters (theological) thinking. Is faith itself or the community of faith a context? Certain traditional ways of understanding theology would say no. On this account, theology (or theological thinking) mediates (applies, correlates, judges) between the authoritative givens of faith and various contexts. According to this interpretation, scripture, tradition, dogma, revelation and the like are not contexts but the authorities by which the community of faith lives in and judges contexts.

I would suggest an alternative view. Even as the theologian is contextual by way of location and situation, even as such things as gender, ethnicity, nationality, language and economic system render the theologian biologically and culturally specific, so is the theologian contextual by way of participation in a community of faith. I shall leave aside at this point the complicated problem posed by those who struggle with theological issues posed by religious faiths but without such participation. For most theologians the community of faith is never merely distant background. Insofar as it has created identity, it is a facet of the theologian's location, and insofar as it is an actual living institution, it influences the situation of the theologian. Furthermore, as part of the theologian's situation, the community of faith functions in theological thinking in both senses of context. First, it influences the life, identity and situation of the theologian. Second, it presents certain elements of its past and present for the theologian to select, weight and attend to in the task of thinking. It should be evident that the community of faith as a context has a certain inevitable primacy over other contexts for the theologian. This is not because the community of faith is on a higher scale of importance than, let us say, the theologian's gender, ethnic group or political situation, but because the undertaking under consideration is theology. It is the community of faith with its perplexities, issues and even high crimes that gives the thinking its theological character.

There appear to be three recurring, some might argue constitutive, elements of the community of faith as a context, that set tasks and provide resources for thinking: the religious traditioned past, the problematized past and present, and the victimized present. Even as thinking presupposes and draws upon a cultural and linguistic past, so theological thinking requires a *religiously traditioned past*. Without the religiously traditioned past persisting into the present in the form of remembered events, texts that attest to origin, creeds and confessions, liturgies, casuistries, church polities and narratives and symbols, theology has nothing to think. Theologians will debate the role and importance of each of these elements in theological thinking. Is some aspect of it, a set of texts for instance, authoritative? Is the religious past reducible to the writings of the two-testament bible? Does this past have a historically relative character? Is it subject to criticism? Does it have constitutive and unalterable expressions, the reiteration of which defines the task of theology? However theologians answer these questions, their thinking cannot avoid dependence on the religiously traditioned past. In this sense the religiously traditioned past is one part of the theologian's situation. Once the theologian incorporates that past into a project of thinking, it becomes a selected and weighted context.

The *problematized past and present* is also a perennial aspect of the theologian's situation and for a variety of reasons. Religion itself embraces and perpetuates the oppressive social stratifications of its time and place and sometimes draws on its own narrative to legitimate those stratifications. Furthermore, religion as a specific, historical institution cannot avoid ways of using human language and creating institutions that finitize, literalize and tame the holy. Prophetic criticism of such things problematizes the recurring idolatries of literalism, chauvinism and ethnocentrism. Religion's past then is always and already a problematized past.

Religion's past becomes problematic in a second way. In certain historical times, a religion may succeed in isolating itself from what may be called the broader world of human culture, knowledge and discovery. This has not been possible for the text or scripture-based religions, dependent as they are on textual recovery, translation and interpretation. Hence one strand of Christian history has appropriated a variety of hermeneutic resources that introduce multiple exegetical and interpretive disputes in the religious community. A third way the faith community's past becomes problematic originates in its commitment to the one Maker of Heaven and Earth. Because of this commitment, faith and the world of faith cannot be simply opposed to or utterly isolated from 'heaven and earth'. There cannot be two truths, the truth of an evil or demonized world, and the truth of faith. Committed to the world as the creation and theatre of a divine activity, the faith community is ever impelled to relate its message to the world-views, ethical claims, aesthetics and politics of the broader culture, and with that, criteria, texts and traditions enter and shape the religious community, often rendering its interpretations problematic. This happened when the religious community's Ptolemaic cosmology confronted the new Copernican cosmology of the Renaissance. These problematized elements of the past linger in the background of all Christian theologies. They become a context when the theologian self-consciously responds and attends to certain of these problematizations. The problematized past and present has been part of theological thinking under the rubrics of faith and reason, natural theology, theology and science, faith and culture, feminist critiques and countless other matters.

The *victimized present* has always been an element in the religious community's situation. The religious community as an imperilled minority can experience victimization. If the religious community becomes culturally established and a cultural majority, it may persecute individuals and selected groups (heretics, witches, women, homosexuals, people of colour), or it may participate in the various ethnocentrisms and racisms of the broader society, discriminating in open or passive ways against slaves, Jews and other religious groups, minorities, even the poor. Even as the religious community itself engenders critics of its own tradition, so it inspires those who adopt the cause of the imperilled victim. Here too we have an intrinsic and enduring strand of the religious community's past that is part of the theologian's situation. This strand, the victimized present, becomes a context when the theologian self-consciously adopts it as an important element in theological thinking.

If the foregoing analysis has any plausibility, theological thinking has never been simply the interpretation or application of the community authorities (revelation, scripture, dogma). The mesh of the traditioned past, the problematized past and present, and the victimized present has always provided theologians with the problems, references, resources and means of thinking. This implies that, however primary the religious community is for theology, theological thinking is never enclosed in the religious community. The reason is that the community itself has never been sealed off from all sorts of issues, criteria, customs and beliefs that enter into and function in the community from its social environments. This holds as much for the Israelite and early Christian communities of canonical times as for present-day churches.

These three contexts do not present themselves to theologians simply as three items on a list. The theologian does not have the option of selecting one of them to the utter exclusion of the others. The most obvious reason for this is that the three are already entangled, already mutually dependent when the theologian takes up the task of theology. Thus liberation, feminist and Third

World theologians utterly committed to social change represent groups that in themselves have a religiously traditioned and problematized past. In addition to being closely interdependent, the three contexts are related by serious ambiguities and tensions. One source of tension is that theologians of the past and present cannot avoid prioritizing one of the contexts over others. It may be the case that if the project is *theological*, the traditioned past always has priority because it provides the narrative resources, orientation and criteria for theological thinking. Even if that is so, one of the other two contexts may set the primary issues and tasks of a specific theological project. This prioritizing has, in fact, differentiated theologies into the types and 'schools' of theology with which we are familiar. The liberation theologian prioritizes the victimized present: the philosophical theologian the problematized past: the confessional theologian the religiously traditioned past.

Tension and ambiguity between the contexts shape theological thinking for another reason. The religious community's normative or ideal references (gospel, kerygma, revelation, scripture, dogma) are present only in modes of interpretation. They never have the status of mathematically clear, analytic or a priori and universally self-evident propositions. There is a density and mystery about them. The ideal referents (criteria) are present in the religious community as historically originated complexes of meaning: that is, as narratives, metaphors, events, personages and so on. These things are themselves interpreted entities, and they pose interpretive tasks for each new generation. If the theologian wishes to critically assess a certain interpretation that has prevailed in the faith community, they will consult a variety of resources (rhetoric, linguistics, social sciences, philosophy, history) to assist the reinterpretation. Because any specific interpretation of the ideal references cannot avoid being culturally specific, errant, incomplete and partially obscure, interpretation in the traditioned past is bound up with the problematized past; hence it poses new critical tasks of interpretation for each generation.

The religiously traditioned past, the problematized past and present, and the victimized present have been present in some form throughout the centuries of Christian theology. Insofar as theologians adopt the paradigm of theology as a science, they will tend to think of these three contexts as elements of method. On the other hand, if theology is a thinking or set of thinkings, each of the three elements will call forth a type of thinking: thinking-from, thinking-towards, and thinking-on-behalf-of. Thinking-from has the character of retrieval and is closely bound up with interpretation. It would re-establish, make sense of and apply an already formulated narrative, symbolic or conceptual tradition. Thinking-towards takes up various items in the background and situation of the community of faith: the universe, language, other faiths, culture and history. Thinking-on-behalf-of arises from an intense awareness of an imperiled group or entity: the natural environment, an ethnic group, a gender, an economic class, children or the aged, a nation, religious community or village.

It is not only appropriate but also inevitable that a theological project involves all three types of thinking. Thinking from the traditioned past, relating that past to aspects of one's location or situation, and commitment to an embattled group or cause are not easy to suppress in any project concerned with what is true and real in the world of faith. Furthermore, there are intrinsic interrelations between these three thinkings that make it very difficult to isolate them from each other. Thus the way the theologian understands the nature of history, narrative and interpretation will shape how they will think from the traditioned past. It is also appropriate and inevitable for a specific theological project to prioritize one of the thinkings over the others. Accordingly, thinking-on-behalf-of will have priority in liberation or feminist types of theology, thinking-towards in philosophical theology, and thinking-from in confessional theology.

The above triad of contextual thinkings does not, however, exhaust theological thinking. Genuine thinking is an act of human self-transcendence, one of the ways human beings break the hold of causalities, influences and even their own 'nature', situation and location. Breaking this hold, they are able to think against: that is, to query, reject, expose and find flaws. Thinking-against can be in the service of thinking-from (confession) and thinking-on-behalf-of, but it can also critically turn against all three contextual thinkings. In addition, authentic thinking is always a thinking-past. Both Catholic and Protestant scholastic theologians debated whether theology was primarily a knowledge (*scientia*), a wisdom, a prudence or an art. The many thinkings of theology suggest it is all of these things. As an art theological thinking always thinks past whatever is given, even the powerful commitments and motivations of confessing, relating to and transforming the world. As an art theological thinking is never mere repetition, the wooden following of a method, or tracing lines of inference. Everything that exists changes, including the theologian's situation, commitments and discerned problems; thus theological thinking always presses into new territory.

The first section identified three meanings and also facets of context: background, situation and location. The present section has identified three specific contexts (influences, settings) of the faith community – the religious traditioned past, the problematized past and present, and the victimized present. What is the relation between these two? The triad of shaping influences that constitute the community of faith specifies that which gives thinking its theological character. As such it describes a dimension of the theologian's context that shapes the theologian's identity (location) and provides resources and tasks for thinking. Thus theological thinking is 'contextual' not simply when it departs from the community of faith into something else, but when it thinks from a traditioned past, thinks towards what has become problematic, and thinks on behalf of those who are victimized, all within a selected problematic of situation, background and location. As a thinking in which non-ecclesial contexts and ecclesial contexts are bound up with each other, theology is an ecclesial, contextual thinking. Nor are the criteria for such thinking simply the authorities of the community of faith. Once the theologian thinks in and towards political, aesthetic, historical or even cosmic situations, a large variety of evidences become appropriate to understanding the working of these spheres.

My Context

I begin this account of my own contextual thinking with two preliminary observations. First, why human beings do what they do, their decisions, acts, preferences and thinkings, is never simply apparent, available to exhaustive explanation. Accordingly, a theologian never knows in an exhaustive way why they responded to some kinds of problems and not others, inclined towards a particular kind of scholarly specialism and thinking, or adopted a specific paradigm of knowledge and evidence. Even after one's personal idiosyncrasies, biographical influences and social locations are identified, many if not most of what provoked the theologian's thinking remains tucked away in the mesh of DNA, self-transcendence, creativity and even the dynamics of self-promotion. Hence this account of the way contexts have shaped my thinking is at best partial and at worst even misleading. Second, constructive theology proceeds not through research but by way of contextual thinking. This thinking is, however, informed, stimulated and corrected by research. Because of the demands of teaching plus the contribution of research to contextual thinking, I expended more effort in research than to contextual thinking: that is, to various studies in the history of philosophy and theology, continental philosophy, social sciences and the arts. When I review the published record of my own contextual thinkings, I find that much of what is at work in those thinkings, especially the interrelation of the contexts, eludes me. I cannot pretend that some overall, pre-planned agenda guided me towards various problems, interests and projects. Thinking itself tends to derail such idealized and totalistic agendas.

My Problematized Past and Present

I begin with the context that I gave priority to, the problematized past and present. To say that I prioritized this context is not to devalue the inescapable importance of the religiously traditioned past. Participation in the religious community was autobiographically prior to my theological projects and always presupposed by them. My theological education and early theological projects took place after natural theology had been discredited (by neo-orthodoxy) and prior to the advent of various praxis theologies. Paramount, therefore, was the awesome legacy of the great Christian theologies of the past (Catholic, Protestant, Protestant liberal) and the tensions between them. This legacy fascinated me and drew me into centuries-old theological issues. At the same time, I became more and more aware of the unclarities, elusive concepts and what sometimes seemed like plain nonsense of the popular religion of my own religious community. This awareness intensified the more I tried to be clear about what the religious community was claiming to be true. My community's ways of citing and using Scripture had become unviable to me, especially after exposure to historical ways of studying the Bible, and the alternatives offered by the prevailing neo-orthodoxies of the day were also unclear and unpersuasive. Does one establish the claim that God is omnipotent by citing a passage in Isaiah or Paul? The assumption behind this quasi-fundamentalist approach was that the beliefs of Scripture writers were in some a priori sense true.

Here the question of the 'reality' of the matters of faith becomes the question of what the Scripture texts say. Theology is simply exegesis and, if something beyond that, applied exegesis. If a historical approach to Scripture overturns the paradigm that makes this notion of theology work, then theology faces a new and very different problem: how does the real enter the life of faith and how does that entry provide a basis for judgments? Two ways of solving the problem were early on closed off to me. It did not help to take the claims (doctrines, symbols, figures) and translate them into a universal conceptual system, a metaphysic if you will. Even if a Platonic, Hegelian or Whiteheadian system were plausible and persuasive, there could be no identity between its very formal or totalistic concepts of knowledge, being or process and what faith called God, evil, redemption or the Christ. Nor did it help to say that the matters of faith were the secluded lore of the religious community, occupants of a fenced-off social mind or idiosyncratic discourse with its own rules, logic, references and stories. That simply gave the religious community itself the status of being a new and unassessable 'scripture'.

My Religiously Traditioned Past

Even though the problematized past in the form of the relativity and errancy of traditional authorities was the paramount element of the ecclesial context, it remained clear that the religiously traditioned past was necessarily prior to and the condition of all theological work. Whatever else theologians do, they cannot but think from the traditioned past. Only such a past could store, mediate and deliver the life-changing message, narratives and symbols so determinative of the community of mutually committed people in which faith had its origin.

To understand this mediatorial function was my first constructive effort (*Ecclesial Man*, 1975). But a social and descriptive phenomenology of how tradition works in the ecclesial community does not answer the question of how the real enters the life of faith and how judgments can be made about it. Again, it became clear to me that what the religious community mediated was not just the traditioned past, the lore of prophets, apostles, bishops and doctors of the church, but what brought about faith itself, namely redemption (freedom, liberation, salvation). Apart from actual redemptive transformation that is ever actual and present in the religious community, the lore or tradition is simply historically relative, the doctrines either conceptualizations of the ancient lore or rootless speculations, the corrupted behaviour of persecution and oppression overwhelming. These issues reduced to a simple question. Did an individual and communal life changing and liberating redemption actually take place in the religious community? If it did, if redemption was something actual at present and not just a memory or a possibility, that actuality was what made everything else work. Some reference was always already there that gave guidance and criteria to assessing the many strands of tradition, identifying the ideal character of ecclesiality, and providing some orientation (a hermeneutic?) for the use of Scripture and other 'authorities'.

Theologians inevitably and properly think from the religious traditioned past, but what gives that thinking its importance and task and prevents it from being an antiquarian curiosity is that an actual, life-changing redemption is ever at work in the present. (I think the same general point holds for the members of other communities of faith who would think from their traditioned past. They too are antiquarians or speculators if there is no actual and available life-changing actuality at work in their community: Jewish, Buddhist, Islamic, and so on.) If this redemption has been found narrative and thematic expression in the origin and subsequent history of the ecclesial community, this sets the task of showing how such narratives and themes took shape from and around that redemption. This task I labelled 'theological portraiture' (*Ecclesial Reflection*, 1982).

My Problematized Past and Present Once Again

From its period of origins to the present, multiple self-understandings, multiple interpretations of Gospel and faith, have constituted the Christian movement. And from the beginning to the present, that movement not only enacted unspeakable cruelties but also held on to all sorts of vague, disputable and even mythological beliefs. In other words, the Christian movement was never a mere ideality but an actual historical entity. Further, the Christian movement defended many of these tenets and actions as absolutely necessary for faith and salvation. And it could attach itself to geological, cosmological and other beliefs that turned out to be scientific nonsense. At the same time, the Christian communities, like their Hebraic and Jewish predecessors, gave rise to prophets and teachers who opposed cruelty, and subjected tenets, metaphors and practices to serious criticism.

The Christian movement, then, is one in which its most definitive and unifying commitment, the Gospel itself, is ever multiple, interpreted, disputed and revised. Accordingly, the Christian movement and its communities present to the theologian two quite different faces: an ideally portrayed and relatively coherent group of narratives and themes that (if it can be shown) express in some way redemption's actuality, and an ever-changing history of disputed interpretations of these very things. These two faces of the Christian movement, ecclesial and redemptive, and the problematized past of ecclesial fallibility and disputation, together constitute a context in which thinking-from and thinking-towards are intertwined. What is the character of this entanglement?

Theology's Appropriated Thinkings

Insofar as we aspire to 'theological method', we open ourselves to questions of 'theology and': theology and philosophy, theology and reason, theology and the sciences, theology and the arts. Herewith we must decide whether theology is compromised if it relates itself to these 'others', to their histories, approaches, categories and values, and whether it must imitate or appropriate their methods. If theology is a complex of contextual thinkings, there is another possibility. In my review of the tensions between the religiously traditioned past and the problematized past and present, theology appeared to be caught in endless and irresolvable disputes. The way beyond this overwhelming plethora of tasks is to recall the theologian's primary task, the thinking of the real and the true in matters of faith. In confessional mood, the theologian is prone to expound the preferred texts: for instance, Paul on the bondage of the flesh. Once the exegesis is done, how does the theologian determine, discern or express the reality of this textual motif? One option is to say that Paul's notion of the bondage of the flesh is real and true because Paul said it, because it is present in Scripture. Such a move provides a reason *why* the motif is real and true (it is present in an authoritative text) but not the specific meaning of its reality and truth. At this point some theologians would move beyond this foundationalism of the exegetical by attempting to locate a parallel between contemporary experience and what the text is about. I have explored another way.

The bondage of the flesh is for Paul an un-freedom that afflicts actual human beings. If this un-freedom is not merely an abstraction, empty of contents, but something that actually alters what human beings are and do, something at work in their actual lives, then the seat or nucleus of its reality is the way it enters and modifies the structure of the self or the ways human beings relate to each other, and even create institutions. If this bondage is not simply a medical condition, a virus of some sort, but something that affects the dynamics and ways of being human, then analyses of human self-transcendence, elemental desires and ways of being social should help us understand just how it alters and distorts the human being. Thus the road to grasping and expressing the exegetical as real and true requires explorations of the complex and dense entities and situations that such things as sin and redemption invade and transform. Travelling this road to the real and the true calls for uncovering the way the theological motif (for example, bondage of the flesh) enters and alters the actual psychological and social field of the human being. The drama or narrative of the Gospel is about how certain powers (such as sin and redemption) enter into and either distort or transform what is already humanly in place. If the theologian is uninterested in this alteration or fails to grasp it, they will miss the specific sense in which the thematics of faith can be actual, real and concrete.

If the theologian takes up this task, they will need to go beyond simply thinking-from (thus from Paul or from the *Nicene Creed*) to a thinking-with other thinkings. The theologian will need to 'think' the structure of the human self, the social and intersubjective constitution of the human beings and the way institutions work. In other words the theologian will appropriate other thinkings in order to expose what is real and true about the religiously traditioned past with its legacy of problematizations. This appropriation is not an abandonment of thinking-from (confession) or thinking-towards. It is not a compromise or dilution of past texts because its aim is to move beneath the level of abstract citation. It is not simply an application or making relevant. It is not correlation, correlating one science, method, or view of things to something in the world of faith, or correlating even something about the human self or situation to a religious symbol. It presupposes that what the narratives of the traditioned past are about is always already bound up with the actual world, actual history, nature, institutions and the enduring marks of the human. Correlation tends to come with the concern for method and the problem of theology and because the matters of the world of faith participate in the world itself, the whole range of the human, the historical, and the natural, the appropriations of other thinkings will never be reducible to a single thinking – philosophical, for instance. Nor will they be reducible to the thinking of a single philosophy. Some philosophers help the theologian think about metaphors and human linguistic behaviour, some (Whitehead) about nature and process, some (Schutz) about human sociality. This is why theological thinking is disciplinarily and philosophically pluralistic. Insofar as any and every theology needs to appropriate non-theological thinkings for the exploration of the real and the true, such appropriation is not a theological idiosyncrasy or even scholarly specialism. The cognitive style of a theologian may privilege thinking-from or thinking-on-behalf-of or thinking-against. But the theologian's work will remain abstract and possibly antiquarian if it postpones indefinitely questions of the real and the true. And to take up these questions requires thinking the matters of faith as they actually occupy, alter and find expression in the actual world.

The Victimized Present

The four volumes of constructive Christian theology I wrote from 1975 to the late 1990s gave priority to the tensions between the religiously traditioned past and the problematized past, a mix of thinking-from and thinking-towards. Did this prioritization ignore or efface the victimized present? Were the issues of oppression and social liberation totally absent from this theological project? If the foregoing analysis is plausible, it is very difficult for a comprehensive account of the world of faith to simply exclude such issues. They find their way into theology simply because of the very content of the matters of faith, informed as they are by the actuality of human redemption. If that redemption pertains strictly and solely to individuals abstracted from their social settings, or if it is simply about the afterlife, then the victimized present will have little place in thinking from and about that redemption.

Such a restrictive individualism and futurism appears to be untypical, even rare, in Christian theology. The oppressed, the victimized, the disenfranchised are always a shadow presence in theological projects even if their specific cause is not articulated, and even when the theologian's work participates in and abets the oppression. Faith itself presses the thinkings of theology toward this context for several reasons. My own theological projects attend to the victimized present in three ways. First, (Christian) faith is centred on the fact and actuality of redemption, and redemption is never merely an eschatological postponement but a present transformation. The traditioned past of the faith of Israel through Judaism and the Christian movement contains powerful paradigms of social corruption, redemption and hope expressed in motifs of covenant people, social–political evil, corporate visions of a transformed history, and a universal community (*ecclesia*) of faith. One aspect of this paradigm, voiced especially by the prophets of Israel, articulated the ways the classes, the monarchy, the temple can oppress the poor and risk the welfare of all by aggressive or near-sighted foreign policies. In addition, the world of faith creates a distinctive sociality (*koinonia*), and this way of human being-together effects a redemptive transformation. This paradigm of social redemption has primacy in all of the works of my project. Accordingly, the inter-human (Buber) and the inter-subjective are primary to and presupposed by individual and even societal dimensions of redemption. A certain kind of deep structural human being-together shapes and impels the transformation of both individuals and their social institutions. References to the victimized present occasionally illustrated these explorations, but the plight of specific ethnic communities were not their primary subject. In my judgment it is both legitimate and important for the theological scene to pursue a variety of ways of addressing the victimized present. In a broad sense, all of these ways are thinking-on-behalf-of. My own selection of this context was to interpret and articulate the real and true dynamics at work in the paradigm of redemption presupposed by criticisms of oppression and by visions of justice.

The context of the victimized present appears in my work in a second way. Although I have rarely been politically active in environments beyond my own setting in the university or seminary, the feminist, African–American, and peace and justice issues have always been central and not marginal for me. Like so many of my generation, I experienced and gave attention to two quite contradictory developments of European and North American societies. On the one hand, these societies became over recent decades more ethnically and racially diverse, and with that came a new acceptance of that diversity that replaced many of the traditional social structures that had kept women and minorities suppressed, powerless and invisible. On the other hand, in the same decades an erosion of certain centuries-old social values appeared to be at work in the deep structures of these societies. One of the many meanings of the post-modern pertains to this erosion. These deep cultural values had functioned as the final court of appeal and as the society's social conscience, impelling it to oppose slavery, racism, capital punishment, incivility, sexism, the exploitation and pollution of the environment, and cultural philistinism. Examples of these values or 'deep symbols' are 'reality' (truth), tradition, law, nature, obligation, hope and beauty. Together, they expressed not so much a moral vision as a communal condition of moral visions. When they decline, a society becomes narcissistic, violent, preoccupied with entertainment and 'fun', vengeful, anti-intellectual and anti-aesthetic. Although I make no pretence of being a cultural historian or sociologist, I thought it important to understand and interpret this massive cultural shift. The reason this project (*Deep Symbols*, 1997) was concerned with the victimized present was that this erosion of deep values has widespread victimizing effects, removing, as it does, some of the impelling bases of social criticism and vision.

The victimized past has been present in my theological work by way of a third interest. The seminary and the university, not the congregation or the church judicatory, have always been the setting of my work. Education has been both the locale and the genre of my everyday activity. Struggling year after year with problems of curriculum and pedagogy, it was natural if not inevitable for me to become interested in the problems and possibilities of theological education. Yet my first writings on education, a few years after graduate school, addressed education in the church and its congregations. Those early essays gave voice to two themes that have stayed with me: the perplexing anomaly of congregational education that does not educate, and the notion that theological education should not be limited to clergy and professors but should be the education that adolescents and adults experience in congregations. Education in the church, the seminary and the university is clearly a third way I have taken up the victimized past. How is this the case?

The issue is how redemptive transformation takes place for both individuals and communities. Christian churches, both Catholic and Protestant, have answered that it occurs by way of sacrament and preaching. I have no quarrel with this. Yet these churches have always offered up educational programmes of sorts: catechesis, Sunday Schools, conferences and retreats. The traditional reasons for these endeavours do not seem to be closely connected to the way these faith communities understand the way redemption takes place. Is there a relation between (church) education and redemption?

Few would contend that simply an objective knowledge of the traditioned past and the church's teachings redeems, and few would see church education as simply transmitting that knowledge. The clue to the relation between redemptive transformation and education may be found in one of the tasks of theological thinking, the thinking that would uncover and not just retrieve from the past, the real and the true. Believers not only have what we might call faith; they are called to live in their settings by way of faith. Nor can they do this if faith simply means the retention of certain scriptural or traditional facts: for instance, what Paul meant by 'the bondage of the flesh'. The believer is called to a freedom that is lived, not simply to hold beliefs held as true.

The believer also faces the theological problem ever lurking in any text and its exegesis. In what way is the 'bondage of the flesh' (and other themes of the traditioned past) real? That is, how are these matters bound up with the complex reality of the believer's actual life or the actual life of the society? The believer is always one who would survive, contribute, create and accomplish in the everyday world, and who has been given biological, intellectual and imaginative equipment for these tasks. To grasp in a personal and life-changing way that the motifs of faith alter this actual life calls for the contextual thinkings of theology. And this is just what education in the church must be. Over many years, education can draw the believer into a life of ecclesial, contextual thinking.

Why do I place this theme in the context of the victimized present, a thinking-on-behalf-of? The answer is that a certain victimization occurs, a certain impoverishment and suppression, when education, the shaping of ecclesial, contextual thinking, is withheld from people in congregations. Here too we have a theme that describes, not the victimization of women and minorities or the pollution of the environment, but the prior educational activity that would orient the believer to these issues.

Four rather fundamental convictions, in an older time we would have said 'propositions', have guided this chapter to its conclusion. First, the genre of theological activity, the sort of thing it is, is thinking and not research. In this sense the essay is more about thinking than method. Second, the context or set of contexts that bring about theology and give it its language and initial viewpoint are certain enduring elements of the community of faith. Although always intrinsically interrelated, any one of these elements can be given priority in a theological project. Third, one element, the victimized present, orients the theologian to aspects of the situation and location that have to do with cultural and even ecclesiastical transformation, criticism and reform. Fourth, all theological thinking is contextual, both in the sense that it participates inevitably in a variety of ecclesial and cultural contexts and in the sense that it selects, responds to and prioritizes certain contexts as primary spheres of inquiry. These convictions provide the framework for my account of my own thinking in context. If I were just now starting again, I have no doubt that my responses or prioritizations would be different. The contextual spheres of oppressed groups, the relation between faith (and its convictions) and the ever-expanding and stunning discoveries of science, and the new proximity between world faiths all call for compassionate, rigorous and creative rethinking. But the problems of the problematized past, especially as they pertain to textual authorities and theological evidences, have not gone away. In fact they seem now to be put aside. In other words the religious, problematized past continues with us and still calls for critical attention. And, as always, the prevailing trends and movements of both churches and theologies ever call to the theologian to think against and to think past.

Chapter 3

Theology in Communion

Colin E. Gunton

The mystery of all lives lies in their contingency: that each of us is born, lives and dies at particular times and places, and these contingencies shape the kind of people that we are. We are formed in, and partly by, our contexts. The contingencies extend right to the heart of Christian theology, for there is at least one respect in which the incarnation, life, death, resurrection and ascension of Jesus are contingent, and yet determine the very essence of the Christian faith. They are historically contingent, for they might not have happened, had God determined otherwise. But they are now necessary, in the sense that, having happened in the way that they did, they determine the shape of the community that lives by their truth. From that a posteriori necessity flows another: that the ministry of the church is an inescapable context for the work of the theologian if it is to continue to be rooted in the historical contingencies that make the practice what it is. Outside of it the discipline of theology becomes rootless and loses its reason for being, however much some recent developments have attempted to evade this fact.

I have begun with these general points because autobiography, though in an enterprise of this kind inescapable, is the lowest and most mendacious of the art forms. And, to begin somewhere near the beginning, of central importance for me was to be brought up in a church of which my parents were active members and teachers, a gift of incalculable worth; and, moreover, one where both family life and churchly education were steeped in the words of Scripture, as well, it is worth adding, as in the context of a love of literature, with Shakespeare and Dickens at the head. To be educated at a school where the Greek and Latin classics were prominent was also a blessing, for they gave entry both into a world which has shaped ours and into the craft of writing, as I now realize on looking back. And, as always, there were the gifts of particular teachers, in lessons on how to work without supervision, on the importance of refusing commonplace answers to questions and, in one case, of an intelligent and enthusiastic Christian faith (allied, it is worth mentioning, to a shared attitude in politics and the fortunes of a local football club). Such particularities as these form us as the people that we are and are incalculable in their long-term significance.

In April 1963, I was in the third and penultimate year of Oxford 'Greats', going with some enthusiasm through the mill of the then almost universally – certainly in Oxford – regnant linguistic philosophy. This created both excitement and anxiety, for although there was theoretically a movement out of the arid positivism of A.J. Ayer into a view where the language of particular fields was to be analysed for its own sake, much analysis of theological language remained reductive, as in the, as we now realize, over-discussed theory of the 'blik'.[1] And then a book appeared. J.A.T. Robinson's *Honest to God* breathed a passion for systematic theology, which was for the most part absent from mainstream English discussion. By 'systematic' I mean something concerned with the meaning of the Christian faith that also engaged with the philosophical mind: indeed, as I now see, more broadly with the mind that more generally had been shaped by not only the Enlightenment, but by Greece, Rome and Augustine. My encounter with a type of theology less determined than Robinson's by modern rationalism still lay a year ahead, and at this stage the book provided an introduction to the excitement of theology – to a feeling that here are indeed questions to be engaged of far greater weight and depth than the often ahistorical orientation and often essentially trivial concerns of much of the philosophy in whose mysteries, if that is not far too strong a word for an essentially arid movement, I was being initiated.

Training for ordination in the second half of the 1960s was an odd experience. There were a number of negative influences, now, in retrospect, appearing mostly rather trivial: 'secular' theology based on a misuse, though one encouraged by the forms of thought, of Bonhoeffer's *Letters and Papers from Prison*. Paul van Buren's poor *The Secular Meaning of the Gospel* was influential, but was also soon to be taken apart in a seminar in the university. But the positive influences of my particular context were greater. One was the weekly sermon class, presided over by the sometimes irascible but also humble – all too aware of his need for grace – John Marsh, whose critiques, far more profound and so more encouraging than those of my contemporaries (from which no doubt salutary scars still remain), taught that most essential lesson of all, that sermons are to be good news; not morals (though they should derive), nor the 'challenge' beloved by earnest young preachers, but good news of the grace of God. To this was added the wonderful teaching, especially lecturing, of George Caird, whose knowledge and love of Scripture outweighed all the destructiveness of many of the biblical critics, and whose teaching still shapes many of those who were inspired by it week after week.

It was once said by John Clayton that it is of the nature of one's doctoral research to set the frame and agenda for the way in which questions are thereafter approached, and so we come to another crucial contingency. Returning to the academic world after a year's almost entirely non-theological activity, virtually the only idea I had was that I wished to research in systematic theology, and, if possible, to teach it. I was awarded a scholarship without the need to specify the first thing about a project, and so simply followed advice, which was to look at one of the then current writers who were making an impact, like Moltmann – whose *Theology of Hope* had recently been translated – or Schubert Ogden. Ogden, along with John Cobb it was, and then Hartshorne, the proposal being to work backwards to their common source in Whitehead in a thesis on Process Theology's doctrine of God. But revulsion intervened (I had been taught too well to be long content with what must be described as sentimental rationalism) and a piece of supervisory genius led to a change of direction which yet enabled the first few months' work to be incorporated.[2]

Robert Jenson was at that time all too briefly in a post in Oxford, and to him I had been allotted. He was writing a book on Barth, and observed that there were parallels between his theology and that of Charles Hartshorne. Both drew on the opening chapters of Anselm's *Proslogion*; both introduced into their doctrines of God a central element of 'becoming'. (Jüngel's important study of Barth's doctrine of God, *Gottes Sein ist im Werden* had recently appeared.) The study took off, with a number of results, the first being a range of illuminating insights about the relations between two worlds that were, on the face of it, virtually incommensurable. What had the allegedly irrational Barth and the rationalistic theologians of process, the denier of the theological propriety of 'natural theology' and some of its enthusiastic proponents, in common? And so the agenda was set, and a concern with the nature of God and the way he is known and named or described has been a constant concern ever since.

An education in the history of Western theology, by the time-honoured method of teaching it, was the next crucial contingency. A post in the Philosophy of Religion at King's College, London, then doctrinally in the grip of a kind of modernist high Anglicanism, 'happened' to be that which turned up, after two years of doctoral research, in 1969. To be set the task of teaching the history of mediaeval and modern Western philosophy is a gift of great value, for the study itself wonderfully complemented the completing of the doctorate, which took a number of years. (Appointment to a university post without a doctorate was more usual in those days.) What became all too apparent – and an invitation to contribute a paper on Polanyi to a conference in 1978 confirmed and deepened some of the insight – was that Western philosophy during and after the Enlightenment was in fact largely a form of theology, as its anti-theological outcome in Feuerbach and Nietzsche made all too apparent. But it was in large measure a theology which had come to represent a heretical or distorted form of the Christian doctrine of creation, in particular, by making the empirical and rational determinants of knowledge antithetical to one another, falling to one side or another of the narrow path along which both the meaningfulness of our world and its material character could be held together. A further aspect of the modernist heresy became more apparent as time went on: that the quest for a purely secular foundation for knowledge amounted to a human attempt to displace God as the source of being, meaning and truth.

These concerns were to give rise to a number of studies of theological rationality in the years ahead, one of them a direct engagement with the theology of the Enlightenment.[3] But in the meantime, Christology was in the air, in the form especially of a number of works that rejected the orthodox confession of Chalcedon. An attempt to salvage Chalcedon in a single paper led to a realization that it needed a book to do so, if such an enterprise was justified at all. (We in theology are not merely concerned to salvage the past, so much as to build on it in order to state the truth of the Gospel in the present, a lesson of which Barth is a great teacher.) Instrumental in the decision was a remark by Dr Geoffrey Nuttall, surely one of the too little sung heroes of English theology. Nuttall, then a teacher of Church History at New College, London, had never heard a paper or lecture of mine in those early years without sending me within days a hand-written critique, without fear or favour saying exactly what he thought – and often overturning my own judgment on the matter. Rarely can a young theologian have received so salutary a gift, and I am by no means the only one to have received it. Writing *Yesterday and Today*,[4] over a long period, scarcely allowable in the context of today's ridiculous pressure on young academics to publish before they have had time to mature, had something of the value of the German system of *Habilitation*, for it required engagement with the history of theology, and especially the Fathers, that had not yet been possible. It is worth mentioning that a criticism by Dr Nuttall of that very book led ultimately to another study of Christology, in which an attempt was made to do more justice to the pneumatological determinants on the doctrine of the person of Christ.[5]

Further engagement with the theological tradition became necessary with an invitation, about ten years into my time at King's, to move sideways into systematic theology. All students then took a course that involved not only Christology but also the doctrines of the Atonement and of the Trinity, the teaching of the latter two enabling other gaps in learning to be filled, insofar as they ever can. For that is the one lesson that theologians must learn: so long as we live, there is more to be learned of and from the astonishingly rich tradition in which we stand. Systematicians are not primarily historians, being concerned essentially with the contemporary statement of the faith of the Church; and yet they need to be deeply conversant with all the theology they can, and especially with the classic texts of the Fathers, the mediaevalists, the Reformers and the moderns. Without the Fathers in particular we fail to come to terms with the essentials of the faith, for it is beyond doubt that those who do not know whence they come soon fall into equivalent errors to those the Fathers fought. This is not a matter of theory, of 'mere' orthodoxy, but of confessing that without which the Gospel is no longer the Gospel, whose distortion stunts rather than enhances the life of those who would live by the faith once for all delivered to the saints.

Distortions there will always be, but they are made the greater by the divisions of the church, first into East and West and then between the divided churches of the West after the Reformation. Would the latter have been necessary if East and West had not deafened themselves to the voice of the other? Who can say, but it seems to me likely that the catastrophic form the schism took has much to do with the different paths taken by Trinitarian thinking in the two main streams of Christendom. That is why an invitation to be part of a British Council of Churches Study Commission on the nature of Trinitarian doctrine, meeting from 1983 to 1988, proved of major formative influence. The Eastern churches were well represented, above all by John D. Zizioulas, now Metropolitan of Pergamon, who for many years has been an academic visitor to King's College, and done much to stimulate teacher and student alike. Barth had already shown that the doctrine of the Trinity is not the mere formulary that it has sometimes been taken to be, but the heart of Christian living and thought. Professor Zizioulas and his colleagues demonstrated that there is to be found in the Cappadocian formulation resources which our Western tradition has neglected to its impoverishment. To be sure, if that were the right way to behave, we could point to similar weaknesses in their tradition's theology and polity, but that is not what we primarily should be about, which is to enable our traditions to be enriched by the wealth of our friends.[6]

And that is what has happened, and has shaped much writing since that time. An invitation to give the Bampton Lectures in Oxford in 1992, itself an indication of the ecumenical tendencies of the time, for this was the first series by one from outside the Anglican clergy, provided the opportunity to probe more deeply into the shape of the modern world, reaching beyond the Enlightenment to its roots in the peculiar combination of Greek philosophy and biblical revelation which shapes the whole of Western culture (and that of the Christian East in a different way).[7] Similarly, *The Promise of Trinitarian Theology* is a series of papers seeking to show the central importance of the Trinitarian shaping of any theology or theological enterprise, to whatever particular end it is developed.[8] In similar light more recent work of mine should be seen, with its increasing emphasis on seeking to show that this is not, indeed, a matter of theory, but of a theology which bears upon life.[9] Moreover, this Trinitarian emphasis is not simply a mark of the work of an individual, for it has affected the thought and life of many teachers and students at King's College and beyond.

As the chapter so far should have made clear, in this discipline, as in life, we are very much what we receive, and in King's College I have been blessed over the years with colleagues and students with whom a series of theological conversations has continued to take place. So many could not be named, but one will serve as representative. Christoph Schwöbel, now of the University of Heidelberg, came to King's as Lecturer in Systematic Theology in the spring of 1986, and stayed until he left to move to a chair in Kiel seven years later. Our conversation and cooperation have continued, but the years he was in England proved the most satisfying and formative period of many very satisfying years. It was his suggestion that we form the Research Institute in Systematic Theology to provide a framework for the work of the increasing number of postgraduate students with which we continue to be blessed. Its meetings, which include a major conference every two years, provide a forum in which teacher, student and guest contribute and receive in equal measure. For theology is a discipline best done in communion, in the image of the triune God.

And that leads me to another essential contextual contingency, the ministry of Word and Sacraments in the United Reformed Church, to which I was ordained in 1972, after becoming convinced that the work I was doing in the university was that to which I had been called as an ordained minister. Indeed, ordination took place in the very Anglican chapel of King's College, and Anglicans, lay and ordained, took some part. Most of the years since that time have been spent as associate minister of the United Reformed Church, at Brentwood in Essex, England. This is, in most respects, a very ordinary church, by no means prospering in a worldly sense, with the usual combination of active and rather less active membership. Nonetheless, it is generous and loving, and has taught the lesson that right theology begins here, where the Gospel is proclaimed by word and sacrament and lived out in the company of others.[10]

Notes

1   Antony Flew and others (1955), 'Theology and Falsification', in Antony Flew and Alasdair MacIntyre (eds), *New Essays in Philosophical Theology*, London: SCM Press, pp.96–130.
2   The outcome: Colin Gunton (1978; 2001 2nd edn), *Becoming and Being: The Doctrine of God in Charles Hartshorne and Karl Barth*, Oxford: Oxford University Press and London: SCM Press.
3   Colin Gunton (1985), *Enlightenment and Alienation. An Essay Towards a Trinitarian Theology*, London: Marshall, Morgan and Scott and Grand Rapids: Eerdmans.
4   Colin Gunton (1983; 1997 2nd edn), *Yesterday and Today. A Study of Continuities in Christology*, London: Darton, Longman and Todd, Grand Rapids: Eerdmans and London: SPCK.
5   Colin Gunton (1993), *Christ and Creation: The 1990 Didsbury Lectures*, Carlisle: Paternoster Press and Grand Rapids: Eerdmans.
6   That should not, to be sure, prevent criticism, merely criticism of a merely polemical or self-justifying kind.
7   Colin Gunton (1993), *The One, the Three and the Many. God, Creation and the Culture of Modernity*, Cambridge: Cambridge University Press.
8   Colin Gunton (1991; 1997 2nd edn), *The Promise of Trinitarian Theology*, Edinburgh: T&T Clark.
9   Colin Gunton (2000), *Intellect and Action. Elucidations on Christian Theology and the Life of Faith*, Edinburgh: T&T Clark; and (2001), *The Christian Faith. An Introduction to Christian Doctrine*, Oxford: Blackwell.
10   The subtitle of a recent book, in which Christoph Schwöbel contributed a fine introduction, makes the point: Colin Gunton (2001), *Theology through Preaching. Sermons for Brentwood*, Edinburgh: T&T Clark.

Chapter 4

The Need for a Scientific Theology

Alister E. McGrath

I was born in 1953, the year in which Elizabeth II was crowned queen. It was a momentous event in British history, which seemed to many to speak of a new era of hope and prosperity. The United Kingdom was beginning to emerge from its period of economic stagnation after the Second World War, and signs of recovery were everywhere to be seen. People were speaking of a 'new Elizabethan era', harking back to the glory days of England under Elizabeth I. Like every child baptized in that year, I was presented with a copy of the English translation of the Bible prepared in 1611 by the command of James I, usually known as the 'Authorized Version' or the 'King James Bible'. I often wondered how that Bible came to be produced – and even got round to writing a book on the topic.

Growing up in the countryside of Northern Ireland was a memorable experience, and one that has shaped my thinking more than I dare admit. My family lived for most of their lives in Downpatrick, the county town of County Down. As the name of the town suggests – it derives from the Gaelic words for 'Patrick's fort' – it has a close link with the patron saint of Ireland, who lies buried in the grounds of the cathedral. I was baptized there, and have always felt a certain degree of affinity with this great saint. My childhood memories are tinged with the thought of the undulating local landscape, with the deep green gently rolling hills stretching far into the distance, leading up to the purple hues of the mountains of Mourne in the far distance.

I never had the slightest interest in religion as a young boy, initially regarding it as a waste of time. After I left the local high school to attend the Methodist College in Belfast, I found my attitudes hardening. A growing interest in Marxism led me to the view that Christianity was oppressive and outdated. Like many young people in those heady days of the late 1960s, I believed that a new world lay around the corner. It would be a world without war, conflict or religion. The student revolts in Paris and other events were harbingers of the new age that was to dawn. Few could fail to be excited by such a vision. Like many others, I found myself entranced by the ideas set out by writers such as Theodore Adorno.

At this stage, I was deeply immersed in the study of the natural sciences. My initial inclination had been to follow the family tradition, and enter the medical profession. However, I found the appeal of pure science to be far more exciting, and ended up specializing in mathematics, chemistry and physics. Having obtained top grades in these subjects at A-level, I stayed on at the Methodist College for an additional year, in order to sit the Oxford entrance examinations. Oxford University offered what was indisputably the finest chemistry course in Britain, and I was determined to study there. I was drawn to Wadham College by its outstanding chemistry dons at the time – R.J.P. Williams and Jeremy R. Knowles – and also by the college's reputation for left-wing politics. I still have the letter from Stuart Hampshire, Warden of Wadham College, informing me that I had been awarded a place and scholarship at the college.

Studying chemistry at Oxford was an intellectually invigorating exercise, and I shall remain indebted to those who taught me for the rest of my life. Yet my life was in turmoil. I had discovered that Christianity was rather more exciting and intellectually resilient than I could ever have imagined. I was now determined to bring my Christian faith into direct contact with the working methods and assumptions of the natural sciences. Though tempted to change course to theology immediately, I was strongly advised to complete my studies in chemistry before moving on. In the end, thanks to the unusual conditions of a scholarship I was awarded at Merton College, I was able to gain a doctorate in molecular biophysics and a first class degree in theology in three years.

I then moved over to Oxford's great intellectual rival, the University of Cambridge. I had been awarded a scholarship (the 'Naden Studentship in Divinity' at St John's College) to undertake research in theology, while training for the ministry of the Church of England at Westcott House. My initial intention had been to pursue research in theology and the natural sciences. However, it became clear that I would need to drink deeply of the Christian theological tradition if that research were to avoid being amateurish, superficial and simplistic – a perennial risk of interdisciplinary work in theology, which often gives the impression of being written by theologians who have just about managed to master 'Teach Yourself Sociology' or have sat in on Quantum Theory 101.

In the end, I opted for the model I found in German writers whom I admired, such as Gerhard Ebeling, Wolfhart Pannenberg and Jürgen Moltmann, all of whom had cut their theological teeth through major research in historical theology, and whose subsequent writings in systematic theology were characterized by an informed and serious engagement with the Christian tradition. Inspired by this, I chose to study one thinker (Martin Luther), one doctrine (justification) and one historical period (the Reformation, set against its later mediaeval context) in detail, and found this an invaluable preparation for serious theological reflection.[1]

Meanwhile, I moved to work as an ordained minister of the Church of England in a parish in Nottingham. This was an invaluable experience, not least in that it raised questions in my mind concerning the spiritual relevance and intellectual viability of the dominant thought-forms within Anglicanism at this time. Preaching regularly to a suburban congregation, week by week, convinced me of the need to be able to interpret the Christian theological tradition in terms that ordinary people could understand, and in ways that conveyed its relevance to their lives. Like many others, I began to grow impatient with academic theology, which seemed at times to dismiss the questions and concerns of ordinary Christians, and speak a language that nobody could understand. My natural home is the world of the Christian community of faith, rather than the dwindling ranks of academic theologians, and I have to confess my concerns over the viability of the latter.

Oxford, however, is my spiritual and intellectual home. A landmark in the shaping of my theological mind therefore took place in 1983, when I returned to Oxford as a lecturer at Wycliffe Hall, a theological college of the Church of England with close links with Oxford University. As a member of Oxford's Faculty of Theology, I was able to lecture on topics which excited me, such as the development of Luther's theology. I became the principal of Wycliffe Hall in 1995, and as my first major project secured its full integration with the University as a 'Permanent Private Hall'. In addition to this institutional development and its implications for my role within the university, my personal commitment to Oxford continued to deepen. In 1999, I was elected to a personal chair in theology by the university; and in 2001, I was awarded the degree of Doctor of Divinity. Like many who have settled in Oxford, I cannot see myself as being at home – physically, psychologically and intellectually – anywhere else.

While I have never belonged to any theological gang at Oxford or elsewhere, preferring to plough my own furrow rather than tag along with theological schools or personalities, I remain deeply indebted to the scholarly achievements of many of Oxford's outstanding writers, especially in the fields of the natural sciences, historical theology and literary criticism. No theologian is an island, and I could not even begin to express my gratitude to the Oxford intellectual environment, which is perhaps unrivalled as a stimulus to creative, responsible and informed theological reflection. If anyone wants to take the trouble to understand me, they will have to understand the remarkable intellectual phenomenon which is called 'Oxford University', and the remarkable opportunities for cross-fertilization that it affords at every level.

My initial agenda was to make theology more accessible to the Christian public. I pursued this agenda of *haute vulgarisation* at two levels. The more visible of the two took the form of writing textbooks, aiming at the clear, accurate and accessible introduction of Christian theology to a wide public. The flagship of this enterprise is my textbook *Christian Theology: An Introduction*, now in its third edition, which has been translated into nine languages, including German, Russian and Chinese.

Yet possibly more significantly, I pursued the agenda set out by Antonio Gramsci, in which he sought to identify a role for the intellectual within popular culture, which corrected the many deficiencies of the traditional understanding of the role of intellectuals, theologians included.[2] Gramsci pleaded for the emergence of an 'organic intellectual', an intellectual who would be committed to the community that she served, helping it to crystallize its ideas and translate them into the idiom of popular culture.

These considerations lead to the conclusion that it is important to appreciate the importance of popular culture. Gramcsi's analysis indicates that it is at this level that ideas are shaped, and values communicated. As Richard J. Mouw and others have argued, academic theology has a lot to learn from popular culture, not least because it forces theologians to listen to the grassroots of their community, instead of talking down to them:

> I am insisting that theological reflection must utilize the insights of the entire Christian community; rather than send the laity off to do their own theology, it is important to draw them into a larger process of theological formation. Professional theologians who regularly ignore – still worse, disdain – the spiritual and theological impulses of popular religion are missing out on an important theological resource. Insofar as popular Christianity is the arena in which ordinary Christians are exercising a discerning practical wisdom, a fully adequate theology will attend to their insights.[3]

The organic theologian will see himself as working within the great historical Christian tradition, which he gladly makes his own. Even when he feels he must critique the contemporary expressions or applications of that tradition, he will do so from a deep sense of commitment to the community of faith and its distinctive ideas and values. He will not see his task as imposing alien ideas upon his community, but as being like the householder who brings out of his treasures 'things new and old' (Matthew 13:52), if I might be allowed this biblically focused way of stating the notion of *sentire cum ecclesia*.

By 1996, I believed that I knew enough about Christian theology to begin a serious attempt to relate theology and the natural sciences. Having kept up my reading in the latter, I felt confident enough to embark on a major writing programme. The stimulus to get on with this programme was provided by a lecture I was invited to deliver at the University of Utrecht in January 1997 on 'The Relation of the Natural Sciences and Christian Theology'. Having spent the summer of 1976 researching aspects of molecular biology at the University of Utrecht, it was a particular pleasure to return 20 years later to lecture on a quite different matter. I expanded this lecture into a book,[4] mainly to clear my mind a little in preparation for the larger task that lay ahead.

This was to write a series of works, setting forth an approach to theology that drew upon the working assumptions and methods of the natural sciences. The project, which has the running title 'A Scientific Theology', sets out to plot a trajectory for Christian theology which maintains its academic and spiritual integrity while encouraging a direct and positive engagement with a scientific culture. The work is marked throughout by a sustained and critical engagement with the history and philosophy of the natural sciences, and a passionate commitment to the legitimacy of theology as an academic discipline in its own right.[5]

My role model here was Thomas F. Torrance, unquestionably the greatest British theologian of the twentieth century. A happy by-product of my engagement with his ideas was a growing interest in Torrance as a person. Theologians show a depressing tendency to treat theology as a disembodied intellectual pursuit, and I found it important to affirm that Torrance (like other theologians) was actually a living human being, who connected his theology with his life and work. Researching his biography was one of the more personally fulfilling research projects of recent years.[6] Although I diverge from Torrance at points, there is little doubt that he has provided a decisive stimulus to those wishing to take the interaction of theology and the natural sciences seriously, rather than just play around with vague notions of human religiosity.

The structure of 'A Scientific Theology' makes it clear that this work is primarily concerned with theological method, rather than with specific theological topics. This structure takes the following form.

Nature

This opening volume clarifies the general position to be adopted, before moving on to a detailed engagement with the concept of 'nature', which is of such decisive importance in any discussion of the relation of the natural sciences and theology. 'Nature' is often treated as a fundamental resource for theology, on the basis of the assumption that it is an unmediated and uninterpreted concept. Yet there is a growing and settled view that the concept of 'nature' actually represents a socially mediated construct. Nature is thus to be viewed as an interpreted notion, which is unusually vulnerable to the challenge of deconstruction. The implications of this for a 'theology of nature' are explored, with especial reference to the Christian understanding of nature as creation.

Reality

The second volume in the series deals with the issue of realism in science and theology, and sets out both a critique of anti-realism and non-realism, and a positive statement of a realist position. In the light of this, the nature of a scientific theology is explored, with particular emphasis being placed upon theology as an a posteriori discipline which offers an account of reality. This volume develops the theological potential of the programme of 'critical realism' developed in the writings of Roy Bhaskar, which has considerable potential for Christian theology in general, and for the interaction of that theology and the natural sciences in particular.

Theory

The third and final volume in the series deals with the manner in which reality is represented, paying especial attention to the parallels between theological doctrines and scientific theories. This volume considers the origin, development and reception of such doctrines and theories, and notes the important parallels between the scientific and theological communities in these important matters.

It is not possible to offer a more detailed account of the approach offered in the space available. Although I intend to pursue research and publish in this field for the remainder of my life, these three volumes should be treated as landmarks in the expression of my theological mind.

However, one issue demands further attention, and has played an important role in the shaping of my mind – namely, the debate over realism in both the natural sciences and Christian theology. The concept of critical realism is of especial importance to my theological agenda. It is widely agreed that a new and highly creative phase in the history of critical realism began with the publication of Roy Bhaskar's *Realist Theory of Science* (1975) and a series of books and articles which followed this over a period of some 20 years.[7] This difficult book is increasingly being recognized as one of the most important philosophical works to have been published in recent years, not least because its method can be extended far beyond the humanities and social sciences, including the natural and applied sciences. Bhaskar's work was hailed as marking a 'Copernican Revolution' in the study of the natural sciences precisely because it transcended an increasingly sterile conflict concerning the achievements of the natural sciences, as well as illuminating the classic conflict between empiricists and rationalists. Bhaskar managed to provide a fresh outlook on these debates largely by attacking the then-dominant positivist conception of science through its flawed understanding of the experimental process. In outlining an alternative, 'transcendental realist' position, Bhaskar allowed critics of positivism to reconceptualize scientific notions such as laws, tendencies and 'mechanisms' without abandoning the notion of science itself.

Bhaskar's approach was taken further in 1979 through the publication of *The Possibility of Naturalism*.[8] On the basis of his realist account of science, Bhaskar offered a fresh perspective on the question of whether social and natural objects can be studied in the same 'scientific' manner. Perhaps most significantly, Bhaskar laid a resilient foundation for a definitive critique of the hitherto dominant positivist and hermeneutical approaches to the philosophy of the human sciences. Yet Bhaskar's insights – which have been hugely influential elsewhere – seem to have been ignored by theologians, especially by those engaged in the dialogue between theology and the natural sciences. For example, Kees van Kooten Niekerk, writing on the potentially rather significant theme of 'A Critical Realist Perspective on the Dialogue between Theology and Science' in 1998, manages to avoid even mentioning, let alone engaging with, the substantial body of literature resulting from the seminal writings of Roy Bhaskar.[9] This has merely reinforced the perception that the 'science and religion' community has become detached from the debates and resources of the mainline academic community. A similar situation seems to have developed within the theological community, with recent publications overlooking Bhaskar altogether.[10]

Rather than perpetuate this less than satisfactory situation, I decided to engage the mainline debate over critical realism in philosophy, and apply its insights to the issues encountered in the natural sciences and Christian theology. It seems to me that trends in current philosophical reflection on critical realism are capable of embracing all that has been affirmed within the professional community of 'science and religion' writers, while at the same time offering a new stimulus to positive yet critical thinking on the issue. There is clearly a need for a radical reappraisal of existing approaches and paradigms, which is probably best achieved by bypassing the intramural debate up to this point.

This, then, is the major issue that will concern me over the next decade: the formulation, defence and exploration of a 'scientific theology'. Yet there are other agendas that must be pursued. In my view, the most interesting concerns the pursuit of the relationship between theology and literature. Why do theologians not write novels, aiming to express theological notions in a narrative manner? There are excellent philosophical models to hand in the novels of writers such as Iris Murdoch. There are many theologians who have written *about* novels; why not write novels instead?

Notes

1   For the resulting books, see Alister E. McGrath (1985), *Luther's Theology of the Cross: Martin Luther's Theological Breakthrough*, Oxford: Blackwell; (1999), *Iustitia Dei: A History of the Christian Doctrine of Justification*, 2nd edn, Cambridge: Cambridge University Press; (1987), *The Intellectual Origins of the European Reformation*, Oxford: Blackwell.
2   For the analysis, see Alister E. McGrath (2001), *The Future of Christianity*, Oxford: Blackwell.
3   Richard J. Mouw (1994), *Consulting the Faithful: What Christian Intellectuals can Learn from Popular Religion*, Grand Rapids, MI: Eerdmans.
4   Alister E. McGrath (1998), *The Foundations of Dialogue in Science and Religion*, Oxford: Blackwell.
5   Alister E. McGrath (2001–3), *A Scientific Theology*, 3 vols, Edinburgh: T & T Clark and Grand Rapids, MI: Eerdmans.
6   Alister E. McGrath (1999), *T.F. Torrance: An Intellectual Biography*, Edinburgh: T & T Clark.
7   See especially Andrew Collier (1994), *Critical Realism: An Introduction to Roy Bhaskar's Philosophy*, London: Verso. The most important primary sources are Roy Bhaskar (1997), *A Realist Theory of Science*, London: Verso; (1986), *Scientific Realism and Human Emancipation*, London: Verso; (1998), *The Possibility of Naturalism: A Philosophical Critique of the Contemporary Human Sciences*, 3rd edn, London: Routledge.
8   Roy Bhaskar (1998), *The Possibility of Naturalism: A Philosophical Critique of the Contemporary Human Sciences*, 3rd edn, London: Routledge.
9   Kees van Kooten Niekerk (1998), 'A Critical Realist Perspective on the Dialogue between Theology and Science', in Niels H. Gregersen and J. Wentzel van Huyssteen (eds), *Rethinking Theology and Science: Six Models for the Current Dialogue*, Grand Rapids, MI: Eerdmans, pp.51–86.
10 See the rather disappointing essay by Sue Patterson (1999), *Realist Christian Theology in a Postmodern Age*, Cambridge: Cambridge University Press.

Chapter 5

The Irony of Grace

Wayne A. Meeks

Many readers will be surprised to find me among the 'theological minds' represented in this volume and none more than I, for my work has privileged non-theological descriptions of the early Christian movement. Indeed, I have felt at times impelled to do battle against what seemed a kind of academic imperialism exercised by professional theologians in deciding what constituted adequate forms of exegesis and of historiography. By now, of course, what remains of the hegemony of theologians is so shrunken that I would almost be moved to join them out of mere sympathy. However, there are more serious reasons for me to return to some of the theological questions that drove me in the first place to pursue a non-theological mode of historical exegesis. Hence I embrace the irony of my position here among theologians.

Irony is the *leitmotif* of my story, not the irony of Socrates, for I never needed to pretend to know less than I did, discovering as I did around every turn how little I really know. I mean rather the irony of existence itself, which I now believe to be the very irony of God, the irony of grace.

Born in the 'Black' and 'Bible Belt'

At age four I became both a racist and, though I did not yet know the word, an ironist. Racism was so constitutive of everyday life in the tiny, rural Alabama town where I grew up that it seems odd to speak of becoming a racist. Yet one becomes a racist when one learns to use the pervasive schema of race to one's own advantage. In my case the occasion was one of those trivial arguments that occur between playmates. Most of my earliest playmates were black, for segregation in that society meant separation only in certain specified circumstances. Losing the argument, I trumped my friend by saying, 'You're just a nigger.' Sixty-five years later I still remember his face at that moment and it is the only clear memory from that year of my life. At once I knew that I had broken something irreparably, though it would be many years before I began to understand the depths of self-contradiction implicit in that moment. We lived in a culture in which genuine, if sharply circumscribed, affection and loyalty could exist between persons whose social and economic status, personal security, life chances, and freedom were radically and inalterably at odds.

The church was as prominent an element in the life of our town and taken as thoroughly for granted as race itself. The culture was entirely Protestant (there was one Jewish family in town; the nearest Roman Catholic church was 20 miles away), differentiated into a variety of denominations that roughly corresponded to social class and which differed only marginally from one another in beliefs and practices. That the churches were as segregated as all other public institutions goes without saying, but perhaps it was in the churches that the self-contradictions of the culture were more likely to come to consciousness than elsewhere. At least in my own experience it was the church that eventually, quite unintentionally for the most part, led me to an awareness of our structural hypocrisy.

My family was Presbyterian, having moved up from Methodism when my older brothers found the Presbyterian youth group more fun. Presbyterians were proud of the intellectual dimensions of their faith. The minister I remember best was a Scotsman trained at Edinburgh, whose sermons were filled with quotations from the British poets. The packed shelves of books that filled his study awed me. My father, too, though little educated formally, was a lover of books and had taught me to read long before I was allowed to begin school. Books became, early in my life, a transport to wider worlds. My 'bookishness' won from my classmates a mixture of admiration and disdain, typical of the ambivalence towards the intellect that has always been a characteristic of broad reaches of American life, felt perhaps most intensely in the South. Even among Presbyterians the love of learning had its limits, and the questioning of received truths was rarely perceived as a virtue. Our pre-progressive Sunday school awarded a prize for memorizing the *Westminster Shorter Catechism*, but none for developing one's own ideas. Still, in that rather rigid and attenuated Calvinism there were glimmers of Calvin's own humanism and faint, unconscious echoes of that remarkable essay on the powers and perversions of human knowing with which his *Institutes* begins. The Reformers all possessed a sense of irony, which Protestant scholastics could ignore but not permanently repress.

Our denomination was a regional one, its boundaries defined by the old Confederacy (reunion with the national Presbyterian body would come only many years later). It shared therefore with the South as a whole a more or less embittered commitment to lost causes. The white South was, before the Vietnam engagement, the only region of the United States to have experienced defeat in war and the only part to have endured occupation, as it was still perceived in my childhood, by a victorious enemy. Public celebrations were fraught with contradictions for anyone who cared to think about them. We celebrated the Fourth of July (though we saved fireworks mostly for Christmas) and Armistice Day, for the First World War had re-ignited the militant patriotism of the Old South, but we ignored Memorial Day, which had originally honoured the Union dead of the Civil War. Living with defeat breeds a sense of irony.

Meeting the World

My brothers went off to the army with most of their generation in the Second World War. They would return having seen a much wider world, and though most of their old prejudices were still operative, those prejudices were no longer unconscious or unchallenged. Their generation was possessed by a new urgency to make up for lost time, a keen pragmatism, and a sense of the possibility for change, a new optimism. The white veterans had little understanding of the ways similar emotions were affecting the African–Americans among them, many of whom would first pursue the American Dream by migrating to northern cities and later would invest their energies in the Civil Rights Movement.

Those of us who had stayed home had changed, too. Glued to our radios to follow progress of the war, we learned names of places we had never heard of, and our imaginations took us far away. The world came to us as well. After the turning point of the battle for North Africa, the government constructed in our town a camp to house 7000 German prisoners of war, roughly five times the population of the town itself. We turned out to watch the arrival of the first trainload of prisoners: lines of young men in grey coveralls marched off to the new barracks behind watchtowers and barbed wire. Soon we would become familiar with some of them, brought under guard to collect freight from the railway depot where my father presided as stationmaster, or giving the occasional concert or exhibition of arts and crafts. We puzzled over these often talented and intelligent men, the Enemy. We learned a few words of German. On rare occasions we would be awakened by the sound of machine gun fire in the night, signalling an attempted escape. We would not become fully aware of the fate of the Jews in Europe until the war ended. We stored memories against the day when contradictions would demand accounting.

The church that had taught me the *Westminster Shorter Catechism* and had made me memorize the names of the books of the Bible (not including the *Apocrypha*) in canonical order did not know quite what to do with this larger world. Nevertheless, it could not conceal from me or even from itself its ancient knowledge that the world God loved was vastly larger than our town or our white South or our nation or the victorious Allies. It sent me to regional and national meetings. It introduced me to Christians very different from Southern Presbyterians. It harboured ministers and lay leaders with progressive ideas, who were eager to impart them to the next generation. It fed me the bread and wine of the Eucharist from the hand of a black minister.

The student Christian movement that flowered in the aftermath of the Second World War thrilled me with its ecumenical vision, introduced me to what seemed then radical new currents in theology, and embarrassed me at my own provincialism. On a bus trip from Alabama to an ecumenical conference in Kansas (one of the great triennial conventions of the Student Volunteer Movement) I learned a little about the feel of segregation from below. When the lone African–American delegate on our bus was refused service at a restaurant, the rest of us had to decide on the spot whether to forgo breakfast in solidarity with her or to pretend not to notice. The following year, as president of the Presbyterian student group at the University of Alabama, I helped to organize and host a state-wide meeting which included African–American students (from a segregated Presbyterian college for Negroes). After complaints from certain townspeople, the dean of students summoned me. 'Mr Meeks,' he said, 'if we were to permit this kind of thing, it could undermine our whole way of life.' With more youthful bravado than prudence I replied, 'Yes, Mr Dean, that is exactly the idea.' The year was 1953, and around me the Civil Rights Movement was gathering momentum. A few years later, as a Presbyterian university pastor, I participated marginally in the desegregation of Memphis State University. One of the active members of our group happened to be present when the advisor of the black students complained to a college dean (rather more sympathetic than my earlier interrogator at Alabama) that none of the religious groups welcomed them. The Presbyterian, without hesitation, said, 'We do,' and marched her new acquaintance over to our centre. Many years later she wrote me, 'We had never discussed it, but I simply knew it was true.'

My first international experience, in the summer of 1955, was also under church auspices and inspired by the student Christian movement. Presbyterian students at the University of Texas conceived the idea of ecumenical work camps in Latin America, modelled on the very successful camps sponsored in postwar Europe by the World Council of Churches and the American Friends Service Committee. As a seminarian, I was chosen to lead one of the camps and so found myself with my new bride, a dozen North American students, an equal number of Brazilian students, one French exchange student and my Brazilian co-leader in a *favela* of Rio de Janeiro. The impact of the experience on all of us was probably more durable than the concrete we novice engineers poured that summer. After seminary, a year studying theology at the University of Tübingen (1956–7) and travelling through Germany, France and Italy would further broaden and complicate my sense of the world and my deracination. I would never be quite at home again anywhere.

Out of the Theological Ghetto

For a time, during my years as a pastor (1957–61), the 'biblical theology movement' seemed an intellectual home, particularly in the form that the student Christian movement had embraced. In my college years, popular study books from the SCM taught me the power of the whole Bible when construed as a continuous narrative or drama.[1] In the slogans of the time, that narrative was an account of 'God's mighty acts', of 'God acting in history'.[2] Such a conception of revelatory history had strong resonance with a postwar generation's reflection on the horrors of the Second World War and the anti-Nazi resistance movements and with a variety of emerging forms of social and political activism. For me, it provided categories for thinking about my own struggles as a white southerner within a racist society and about my observation of economic oppression both in my home region and in the southern hemisphere.

When later I began serious reading of Karl Barth's *Church Dogmatics*, it was that same sense of revelatory narrative that captivated me; as Hans Frei explained, Barth read the Bible as the original non-fiction novel.[3] Yet Barth's notion of history was more complex and difficult than that which seemed typically to underlie the biblical theology movement, and his telling of the story was much harder to square with the historical–critical method upon which the movement was founded. The method itself was coming under attack, not only from the right but now also from within the critical guild, though the full assault by post-modernist, feminist and post-colonial critics was yet to come. Hans Frei, earlier my teacher, later my colleague at Yale (from 1969 until his death in 1988), pointed out in his *The Eclipse of Biblical Narrative* that both the modern biblical critics and their conservative opponents needlessly constricted interpretative possibilities by limiting the meaning of texts to their ostensive or referential meaning. That is, they understood words to signify only insofar as they pointed to something 'behind', 'beyond' or 'outside' themselves: a transcendental idea, a dogma, a set of facts, or a 'real' event in space and time.[4] By the time Frei wrote that, however, I was already reading history quite differently from the way the biblical theology movement understood it.

To improve my German while studying in Tübingen, I had chosen two authors for extracurricular reading: Dietrich Bonhoeffer and Franz Kafka. I devoured their works. Of the two, my encounter with Kafka (the master ironist) probably affected my sensibilities more profoundly in the long run but his influence was subtler. Immediately Bonhoeffer's notion of 'the world come of age' captured my attention. In this secular age, Bonhoeffer insisted, the task of theology was not to 'make room in the world for God', as he characterized the aim of liberal apologetics, but to proclaim 'the God who lets us live in the world without the working hypothesis "God"...'.[5] In setting the Gospel against 'religion', Bonhoeffer's debt to Karl Barth was obvious, but Bonhoeffer's critique of Barth's 'revelation–positivism' was sharp and, in my later discussions with Frei, still seemed relevant.[6] What was the relationship between what the biblical theologians called 'salvation history' and the history that ordinary historians wrote, 'without the working hypothesis "God"'? This was becoming an increasingly difficult question to answer, and 'history' increasingly hard to define.

One thing was clear to me: the modern university, however much one might have to qualify the adjective 'secular' when applied to it, was a place where 'the working hypothesis "God"' could not be assumed. In the shape of academic study of religion in the United States, 1963 was a turning point. In that year a decision by the US Supreme Court, remembered principally for its finding that organized prayer in public schools violated the constitutional separation of church and state, declared that there was no legal bar to 'objective' teaching about religion in public institutions.[7] Within a few years many state-supported universities created departments of religious studies for the first time, and not a few of the old private universities remodelled their 'Bible' or 'religion' departments. Consequently, the centre of gravity of the discipline in North America shifted quickly from seminaries and theology departments to these new pluralist departments. The small National Association of Biblical Instructors was transformed in 1966 into the American Academy of Religion, which soon became a huge organization and a forum for vigorous debates over both theoretical and practical questions about the place of religious studies in a multicultural university.

I had committed myself early on to the university as the context of my vocation as a pastor. My second career as a teacher was exercised entirely in departments of religious studies, at Dartmouth College, Indiana University and Yale University. In both roles I found Barth's anti-apologetic stance appropriate. The church and its story could be allowed no special pleading. The story was to be told as honestly as possible, with the view from inside and from outside, as Richard Niebuhr would say, both fairly represented.[8] But what was honest and what was fair?

When a fellowship made it possible for me, after four years in the campus ministry, to return to graduate school in 1961, I applied for a programme at Yale called 'biblical theology'. By the time I arrived in the fall, however, that programme had been eliminated by vote of the faculty, a harbinger, and I enrolled in New Testament studies. More changes were to come. At the end of my second year, the entire doctoral programme was moved from an administrative committee composed almost exclusively of Divinity School faculty into the newly created Department of Religious Studies. It was the same year in which the Supreme Court announced its decision, mentioned above, that changed the face of American public education. Yale's new department, along with only three or four other doctoral programmes in the USA, would dominate the production of new teachers for the departments that would be created thereafter in secular universities. At the time I had no inkling of the significance of these events. I was preoccupied with a vast array of things that needed to be learned, a wife and children on short rations under a graduate student's budget, a book manuscript I had promised before beginning the doctorate, and lingering guilt for being hidden in a library rather than on the front lines of the civil rights struggle.

Even in those circumstances my three years in graduate school were taut with intellectual excitement. My fellow students were bright and engaging and my teachers were extraordinary. The dominant figure with whom we had to wrestle was still Rudolf Bultmann, who was, among other things, the most severe critic of 'salvation history' and the ecumenical theology based on it. With great reluctance I recognized the cogency of Bultmann's criticism. I stood in awe of his exegetical brilliance and the comprehensive scope of his historical synthesis, which placed the origins of Christianity in the context of the history of religions as practised by Bultmann's predecessors and contemporaries. Nevertheless, his existentialist hermeneutics did not satisfy me. It seemed to lead to a dangerous subjectivism, yielding no foundation for social ethics, and it entailed a conception of human identity that I thought simply wrong.

Nils Alstrup Dahl was a visiting professor for my first year (later he would return for 16 years at Yale, for most of which I was privileged to be his colleague). He had studied with Bultmann before the war, but his own approach was shaped by the broader Scandinavian tradition of the history of religions, including the phenomenology of myth and ritual, by a deep and sympathetic knowledge of the Jewish sources contemporary with the emergence of Christianity, and by good Norwegian common sense. Paul Schubert had been trained in classical philology in Germany before coming to the University of Chicago for a second doctorate in New Testament. He pioneered in the stylistic analysis of letter conventions, carefully comparing the theories of letter style in the rhetorical handbooks of the Greek and Roman world as well as the actual practice of the ancients in both literary collections of letters and the hordes of private letters preserved on papyri. In place of the German technical terms 'form' and 'life situation', Schubert borrowed the architectural motto, 'form follows function'. His insight, that to understand religious language one should ask after its function, was to prove prolific for my thinking. The director of my dissertation (which began as a paper written for Dahl in my first semester) was Paul Meyer, whose theological position was very close to Barth, but whose principal influence on me came from the clarity, precision and absolute honesty of his exegesis of texts.

Perhaps the most important thing that happened to me at the beginning of my new career as a scholar was my discovery of Judaism not as 'background' for the New Testament, as most New Testament handbooks still treated it, but as a living family of diverse and adaptable forms of life. In my first semester at Yale I studied with Erwin Ramsdell Goodenough, who introduced me to Philo of Alexandria and to Jewish iconography, demolishing the myth of 'normative Judaism'. Years earlier, as an undergraduate physics major, I had taken a course called 'Introduction to Judaism' with Henry Fischel, then director of the Hillel Foundation at the University of Alabama and later a distinguished professor at Indiana University, where I would be for a short time his colleague. For Fischel the common dichotomy between 'Hellenism' and 'Judaism' in antiquity was absurd. Only another colleague with whom I would later share so much, Abraham Malherbe, equalled his expertise in the Cynic tradition, which he found reflected in rabbinic literature.

Another formative figure was Bernard Citron, who was my first teacher of critical New Testament exegesis at Austin Presbyterian Theological Seminary (1953–6). An outspoken Jewish editorial writer for a Berlin newspaper, Citron had been forced immediately after Hitler's election as Chancellor to flee to Budapest, where he converted to Christianity in a Church of Scotland mission. He taught me to read the New Testament as a Jewish document. At Yale, Nils

Dahl expanded that insight by showing that the *pesharim* from Qumran could reveal the way an apocalyptic sect like the Essenes or the early Christians created eschatological ideology out of the interplay among their reading scripture, revising tradition, and making sense of their own history and circumstances. Judah Goldin in his continuing seminars unlocked the delicate aesthetic of *midrash*. Then at Dartmouth I was for a year a colleague of Jacob Neusner, who was just beginning to turn the world of Jewish studies upside down. For many years he was for me a valuable informant and a generous friend. A few years later I was privileged to be involved in the founding of the Judaic Studies Program at Yale. The process brought me a wide acquaintance with the field and eventually the boon of having Steven Fraade as colleague. This extraordinary sequence of happy accidents could happen only in American universities, and here only in very recent times.

My personal journey was a meander among several broad cultural streams flowing through the university and the society in the late twentieth century. The changes in my understanding of the task of biblical studies can be summarized under four heads. First, attempts to discover the uniqueness of the New Testament and its writers against the 'background' of the Jewish, Greek and Roman worlds have given way to attempts to understand the new movement as a family of diverse ways of participating in that manifold cultural mix. Second, the history of ideas has yielded pre-eminence to social history. Third, synchronic description has taken precedence over diachronic explanation. Finally, for many exegetes one or another of the social sciences has replaced theology as the primary discussion partner.[9]

From Background to Cultural Ecology

Those of us who pursued doctoral studies in the New Testament in the 1960s were generally required to demonstrate our knowledge of the *background* of the New Testament. That requirement was subdivided into the Hellenistic background and the Jewish background. Although we had to know something of both, often we were expected tacitly to concentrate on one or the other, and the choice entailed not only historical but also theological, that is, apologetic assumptions. Few doubted that 'Hellenism' and 'Judaism' named cultural realms that were fundamentally opposed to each other, and the choice to silhouette early Christianity primarily against the one or the other implied opposing conceptions of what true Christianity was about. Perhaps the most massive and complete shift in our approach to the history of ancient Christianity in the past half-century has resulted from our coming to see the varied forms of the early Christian movement not in contrast to that imagined dichotomous background but rather as indigenous developments within an enormously complex cultural matrix.[10]

The change in perspective was twofold. On the one side we discovered how varied were the ways in which Jewish groups adapted to their situation within the culture of the Hellenistic and Roman worlds. An array of evidence challenging the old consensus had been collecting for decades in archaeological discoveries, Jewish iconography, papyri, literary comparisons and new techniques of formal analysis, but it was not until the 1960s that the cumulative weight of that evidence shattered the ruling paradigms. The discovery of the Dead Sea Scrolls beginning in 1947 was probably the most immediate catalyst of the intellectual upheaval, but another essential factor was the relocation of many of the leading scholars of early Judaism and early Christianity from theological seminaries to the humanities faculties of universities. One consequence was that mutual engagement between students of Jewish communities of the Greco-Roman world and students of early Christianity has come to be a routine fact in North American universities and learned societies. I have mentioned above the names of some of the individuals who were most important in my own involvement and a few of the stages in the development of my understanding.

The other side of the coin is that we have had to give up exaggerated claims to Christianity's uniqueness. The more we learned about the wide range of different ways by which Jews adapted to the society of the Roman provinces, the more we recognized similar modes of adaptation in the records of early Christian groups. The Christians looked more and more Jewish. We were prepared for that discovery in part by our moral revulsion at the genocide that modern anti-Semitism had brought forth and at the fact that centuries of theological caricatures of Judaism had fed the modern racial demons. Belatedly we came looking for the Jewishness of Christianity, not in service of supersessionist apologetics, but to correct a distorted history that supersessionism had written.

Yet if the early Christian movement looked more and more like an odd sect of Judaism, at the same time we were discovering more and more family resemblances between it and forms of life common in the larger societies of the Greco-Roman cities. Groups as diverse as immigrant organizations, clubs and professional guilds, magicians and their clients, rhetorical and philosophical schools proved to bear some important similarities to the writers and users of the earliest Christian documents. The world of antiquity did not divide neatly into pagans, Jews and Christians. Whatever was distinctive about the Christian movement was embodied in the diverse repertoire of social idioms shared in the larger culture.

From History of Ideas to Social History

Apart from my friendship with scholars of Judaism, the most important factor in my loss of theological innocence was 34 years of teaching undergraduates at Dartmouth College, Indiana University and Yale University. The best of them were stubborn sceptics, insisting that I make clear to them exactly what it was I was talking about and why I thought it true and why it was important.

Few of the assured results of modernist historicism, fewer still of the kerygmatic appeals of Bultmannian existentialism survived the assaults of their innocent and not-so-innocent questions. I reformulated their questions for myself, in the book in which I attempted the first tentative answers, to ask: 'What was it like to become and be an ordinary Christian in the first century?'[11]

If it was the students who focused my dissatisfaction with the former ways of asking questions, it was a company of colleagues who helped me to a new way of trying to answer them. A conversation with Leander E. Keck in 1972 led to the organization, under joint auspices of the Society of Biblical Literature and the American Academy of Religion, of a working group on 'the social world of early Christianity'. The group, with a changing membership that was always diverse, argumentative and exciting, continued for many years and led me into new ways of working. Most important to my own development as a social historian, however, was the close collaboration I enjoyed at Yale for a quarter-century with two colleagues in particular: Ramsay MacMullen and Abraham Malherbe. MacMullen taught me that the history of the Roman empire was about more than battles and emperors on the one hand and the ideas of the *élite literati* on the other and that by the study of inscriptions and papyri, the shapes and sizes of cities, graffiti and magic spells, and above all by asking the right questions, one could learn about the texture of the social fabric in which ordinary people lived. Malherbe was teaching me and generations of our students how the commonplaces of popular philosophy and rhetoric could be found reflected in the language of the early Christian writings and how those commonplaces, too, opened new windows into that same social fabric that MacMullen and others were exploring from a different angle.

From Diachronic Explanation to Synchronic Description

The 'history of religions' school, which so powerfully shaped New Testament scholarship in the mid-twentieth century, focused its attention on the chain of influences that created the syncretism, the mix of cultures, that constituted the religious atmosphere of the Greco-Roman world and hence of early Christianity. To explain a phenomenon, one sought for its antecedents. The literary counterpart of this search was the quest for the sources comprised by the transmitted documents of the New Testament. For example, Bultmann extracted from the Fourth Gospel a series of earlier documents, one of which was a collection of 'revelation discourses' in a distinctive Semitic style. Seizing on a perceived similarity of this style with some newly translated literature from an ancient baptizing sect called the Mandaeans ('knowing ones' equivalent of the Greek 'gnostics'), still surviving in Iraq and Iran, he constructed a grand solution to the 'puzzle' of the Johannine Gospel. A member of the Gnostic proto-mandaeans, Bultmann reasoned, converted to Johannine Christianity, bringing with him poems that had originally praised John the Baptist as a Gnostic revealer. Transforming the myth of John as a revealer to speak instead of Jesus, that anonymous former Gnostic created the 'riddle' of the Gospel. That riddle could be solved, then, only if one knew the 'powerful myth' that lay hidden behind it, which the author had deliberately broken. By putting the myth back together, with the help of the Mandaeans, one could understand what the evangelist had meant by what he had not said. The brilliance of Bultmann's historical construct is matched by the adroitness of his detailed exegesis. There is nothing else in New Testament scholarship of the twentieth century to equal the grandness and precision of the whole. And yet, as an historical explanation, it does not finally work, as I discovered to my dismay when I wrote my doctoral dissertation on Johannine Christology.

In an essay that became the turning point of my research, I decided to explore another way of understanding myths. Instead of trying to solve the riddle, I thought perhaps one should first ask in what kind of situation riddles could serve as a privileged means of communication. That led me into a number of wild goose chases and blind alleys in the social sciences, but eventuated in the article published in 1972, 'The Man from Heaven in Johannine Sectarianism'.[12] In search of theoretical guidance, I had blundered into the sociology of sect formation, a not uncontroversial field, and into attempts to describe religious phenomena as elements of cultural systems. That is, instead of explaining ideas by reconstructing older ideas that an author had 'borrowed' or which had 'influenced' a new formulation, I sought to understand how religious language and practices worked together in a particular social setting.

A Wary Dialogue with the Social Sciences

My readings in the classics of sociology and social anthropology, in part in graduate seminars with several generations of Yale graduate students, in part with two groups of colleagues in summer seminars sponsored by the National Endowment for the Humanities in 1977 and 1979, showed me how complex were the questions onto which I had stumbled. I found myself most in tune with the work of Max Weber and his successors, though I no longer shared the philosophical idealism implicit in his theory. Weber's was an approach to sociology that aims at understanding rather than explanation, correlations ('elective affinities') rather than one-sided laws of causation between social structure and ideology, a human rather than a natural science.[13] Standing in the Weberian tradition, the discipline of the sociology of knowledge, as defined especially by Peter Berger and Thomas Luckmann, helped me to formulate the issues to be sorted out. The other major contributors to my emerging theoretical perspective were social and cultural anthropologists. The notion of the historian as ethnographer, trying to understand the culture of strangers in a different time as well as a different place, was suggestive, although one had to keep reminding oneself that this notion is a metaphor and that the cases are in fact quite different.

One has only to glance at the programme of an annual meeting of the Society of Biblical Literature to see the extent to which the social sciences now rival theology as a discussion partner of biblical scholars. While I welcome this development and had a small part to play in it, I am more sceptical than many of my colleagues about the wholesale adoption of social scientific theory. What I resist is not so much the 'reductionism' so often decried by theologians, which seems to me at worst no more dangerous than the centuries-long theological practice of reducing the subject matter of religious language to dogmatic propositions; rather, grand theories and the brittle 'models' often derived from them tempt us to *deductionism*: the temptation to deduce from what theory tells us 'people always do' what the first Christians *must* have done. From my early training in physics I retain a certain snobbishness about the 'science' of social science and hence about the quality of social theories. Absent any prospect of a grand unified theory of human behaviour, we are best served by a rather eclectic theorizing that may open our eyes to new ways of asking questions but keeps us close to the evidence and open to the surprises of people who do not behave at all as we expect them to.

Faith's Ironies

In the Bible's stories, it is the principal character, God, who most often behaves in ways in which we, and most of the characters in the narrative, do not expect. It is that quirkiness of God that still captures the attention of a close reader. For me it does much more. The ironies (not to mention the paradoxes and the self-contradictions) of the narrative of God point, I think, to a poetics of faith in which not merely the ironies of my individual life but also the ironies of the history of the peoples of God may eventually make sense. In the face of the vast harm that Christians have done to one another and to others, not merely accidentally or by this or that specific disobedience but often deliberately and carefully while citing quite central elements of the tradition, it would not be possible for me still to be a Christian if it were not for the irony of grace.

Perhaps the greatest test for Christian imagination and faithfulness in the present century is posed by the fact of our having to live in a world the vast majority of whose inhabitants are not and will not ever be Christians. The old answers, roughly speaking, that they must convert or be damned are impossible. What is it that our unpredictable God is doing with these people and saying to us through them? Like many of my contemporaries, I confront this issue directly and personally, for recently, as a widower, I was remarried to a non-believer. Just the other day we attended the marriage of a friend at which the Eucharist was celebrated. The vows stirred vivid memories in us both. Yet the Communion, which the celebrant told us is the sacrament of unity, did not unite us, for she is Jewish, unbaptized and agnostic. Nevertheless, we are, in the biblical phrase, one flesh and, moreover, on most important matters, of one mind. We dare to celebrate this irony and to name the magic of our meeting 'grace'. Is it possible that the church in the new millennium will find places in its talk about God, not just tacitly at the edges but boldly in the centre, to speak of ever new ways in which God is breaking down 'the middle wall of partition' (Ephesians 2:14 KJV)? It may, if it dares to trust the irony of the unpredictable and unnameable God.

Notes

1 For example, Suzanne de Dietrich (1958), *The Witnessing Community: The Biblical Record of God's Purpose*, Philadelphia: Westminster Press; (1960), *God's Unfolding Purpose: a Guide to the Study of the Bible*, Philadelphia: Westminster Press; Bernhard W. Anderson (1953), *The Unfolding Drama of the Bible: Eight Studies Introducing the Bible as a Whole*, New York: Association Press.

2 For example, G. Ernest Wright (1962), 'God Who Acts: Biblical Theology as Recital', *Studies in Biblical Theology*, London: SCM Press.

3 The phrase is actually David Kelsey's, speaking in private communication of Frei's interpretation.

4 Hans W. Frei (1974), *The Eclipse of Biblical Narrative: A Study in Eighteenth and Nineteenth Century Hermeneutics*, New Haven: Yale University Press.

5 Dietrich Bonhoeffer (1956), *Widerstand und Ergebung: Briefe und Aufzeichnungen aus der Haft*, E. Bethge (ed.), Munich: Chr Kaiser, p.241. Bonhoeffer first used the phrase *die mündig gewordene Welt* ('the world come of age') in a letter dated 8 June 1944, just two days after the Allied landing in Normandy, an event that Bonhoeffer had noted in a brief, exultant message on the day.

6 See Bonhoeffer, pp.219–21.

7 'Nothing we have said here indicates that such study of the Bible or of religion, when presented objectively as part of a secular program of education, may not be effected consistently with the First Amendment' (*Abington School Dist* v. *Schempp*, 374 US 203 [1963]).

8 H. Richard Niebuhr (1941), *The Meaning of Revelation*, New York: Macmillan.

9 I have rehearsed these developments in greater detail in the 'Introduction' and 'Afterword' of a collection of my essays in the forthcoming text: Allen R. Hilton and H. Gregory Snyder (eds), *Down to Earth*, New Haven and London: Yale University Press.

10 I have written more extensively about these changes in Wayne A. Meeks, 'Judaism, Hellenism, and the Birth of Christianity', in T. Engberg-Pedersen (ed.) (2001), *Paul Beyond the Judaism/Hellenism Divide*, Louisville: Knox, pp.17–28.

11 Wayne A. Meeks (1983), *The First Urban Christians: The Social World of the Apostle Paul*, New Haven: Yale University Press, p.2.

12 Wayne A. Meeks (1972), 'The Man from Heaven in Johannine Sectarianism', *Journal of Biblical Literature*, 91, 44–72.

13 Reinhard Bendix, 'Two Sociological Traditions', in R. Bendix and G. Roth (eds) (1971), *Scholarship and Partisanship: Essays on Max Weber*, Berkeley: University of California Press, pp.282–98.

Chapter 6

The Last of the Last:
Theology, Authority and Democracy

John Milbank

I

Should theology owe its prime allegiance to the academic community or to the Church? Should it be, as David Tracy advocates, primarily a 'public discourse' answerable to the critical norms and liberal values of free society in the West, or should it be the faith of the Church seeking understanding according to a logic indissociable from this faith, as encouraged by Joseph Ratzinger?

Faced with such a stark alternative, many people are likely to propose instead a compromise. Given that the notion of a contextless reason, without presuppositions and affective practical commitments, is a fiction (as recent philosophy, analytic and continental, has tended to conclude) then it is with and not contrary to reason to suggest that a well-established community and tradition may undertake to articulate its own implicit reasonings. However, if this reflection is not to be merely self-regarding, it must also be subject to critical reflections coming from external sources: for example, the diagnosis of 'ideologies'.

Yet the problem with any mere compromise is that it piles up a double problem and compounds it with contradiction. One is still left with the question of an uncritical solipsism and of the fictional perspective from nowhere. If the two are combined, one is trying to believe at once that reason founds itself and that this is impossible. At this point some theologians have had recourse to semi-Hegelian solutions, often inspired by J. Habermas. Critique is imminent: one must begin with a tradition and assumptions, but a negative process of unravelling contradictions in the first deposit gradually drives towards a universal *logos*.

This solution leaves us in no better plight. Traditions unfold by acts of hermeneutic discrimination as well as by the overcoming of contradictions. Something ineliminably subjective and feeling-imbued is just as involved in development as in inheritance, in continuation as in origin. And, however long the process of formally objective logical negation, this cannot alter the positive status of the beginnings. One remains entirely inside a tradition. Conversely, if a logical process is still the only criterion for socially acceptable truth, one is persisting with placeless, formal and self-founded criteria for reason. The idea that a tradition will edge towards the universal through the outworking of contradiction, or conversely that a foundation will finally emerge at the conclusion, is itself contradictory. So one still has a compromise between two perhaps unsatisfactory positions that sustains the unsatisfactoriness of both and adds to this the unacceptability of downright incoherence.

Is it possible to do better than this? I want to approach this question at first obliquely, by noting that a penchant for compromise also invades the sphere of ecumenism. Very often, documents issued in the name of joint doctrinal statements between different churches produce their results by toning down given differences or glossing over their ineluctable historical reality. So, to give a short example, it will be discovered that Aquinas and Luther have 'essentially the same' doctrine of justification. There can be much truth in this sort of conclusion, given that by Luther's day the nature of Aquinas' account of salvation had been obscured, and that since his day the views of both in this area have been yet further obscured. Yet in the end, an irremovable difference which is significantly linked with their exceedingly different ontologies (realist/ analogical versus nominalist/univocalist) tends to be passed over. Luther's nominalism will not really admit the Thomist paradox of a righteousness that is entirely supernatural, yet also entirely ours since it is our deification. Instead, the younger more 'participatory' Luther is in fact developing the consequences of an almost monophysite (well, actually *more* monophysite really than the formal monophysitism of the monophysites – although John Philoponus at least seems already to have been a sort of nominalist) Ockhamist Christology which cannot really think two universal 'natures' in a single personal reality, nor think this reality other than on the model of a single finite thing 'inside which' God has somehow entered.[1] Within such a perspective, the participation in Christ by which we are justified edges too closely towards mere identity and subsumption. Aquinas' apparently similar Cyrilline tendencies actually have totally different realist logic. Luther's nominalist univocalism finds another solution in his later extrinsicist, imputational account of grace, which is more obviously alien to that of Aquinas.

This kind of upshot in ecumenical documents seems to me to do a disservice to the cause of truth and run the risk of making theology look, indeed, to be biased from an academic perspective. What seems crucial here is that, while ecumenical reflection makes some use of historical research to upset prejudices about what different communities have believed from their outsets, it does not take this process far enough. At bottom it is a matter of developing mutual respect between different ecclesial bodies, not of questioning the very character of these bodies. In this respect, ecumenics is very much conducted on a basis that is internal to received variants of the faith. Yet here a more external, objective approach might be more inclined to ask questions about the common intellectual assumptions of both the post-Reformation and the post-Tridentine faiths, and the possible deviation of these from earlier Christian views.

There does in fact seem to be an increasing consensus amongst historians both of events and of ideas, that neither the Reformation, nor the somewhat elusive 'Renaissance', nor even the later 'Enlightenment' were anything like such crucial shifts in Western theory and practice as the multiple changes which took place before and after the year 1300.[2] Around that year, there started to be a far greater gap between specialists and non-specialists in all fields; administration became more technical and distant; republican/ecclesial civic participation within the Italian city-states collapsed; clerical control over the laity further increased; sharper differentiations were made between academic disciplines; theology assumed a far more technical and difficult character; the traditional centrality in theology of metaphysical participation, deification, apophaticism, allegory and the Church as engendered by the Eucharist all were abruptly challenged in a fashion that proved epochally successful. Meanwhile much that had been taken for granted in the Aristotelian/neo-Platonic synthesis and had been shared with Byzantine, Jewish and Islamic culture, was declared from henceforth unacceptable by the ecclesial authorities. Many historians consider that the later break-up of Christendom was itself in large measure the upshot of these changes, and equally that the same changes already ushered in a drift towards 'secularity'. This has implications both for ecumenism and for the debate about the relationship of theology to secular culture. For sometimes great faith is invested in the possible upshot of Christian reunion, particularly within the 'Yale School' of American theologians: secularization is seen as a negative reaction to Christian disunity, reunification as the key to renewed mission. However, if the new emerging historical consensus is correct, it is rather the case that secularization, not ecumenism, is the prior problem. It might be that Christian division was itself an outcome of a severe weakening of the Christian vision, and that the key to ecumenical discussion would be a far more drastic critique of the character of existing ecclesial bodies.

What I have just said seems, however, to impose too much duality between theology and history. It cannot in fact be an accident that much of the new picture of the history of ideas and of the Church is itself inspired by theologians – but by theologians prepared to be critical concerning the contemporary norms of the ecclesial body to which they belong (overwhelmingly, this body is the Roman Catholic Church).

So far I have tried to interweave connections between debates about theology between the churches, and debates about its respective relations to the Church and to the academic community. We are talking, then, about the sources of intellection in theology, which are frequently taken to be Scripture, tradition and reason. All too often, my own Anglican community has presented itself as having a uniquely balanced orientation to all three loci. This way of understanding the grounds for theologizing is, however, wholly unsatisfactory – in fact it is ultimately an upshot of the 'crisis of 1300'. It tends to result in arguments for the predominance of one of these elements or another, or else for compromise between their respective sways. But the problem with 'tradition', as we saw, seems to be solipsism; the problem with 'reason' seems to be its unreal and impotent abstraction; the problem with 'scripture', one can add, is its magical positivity. Compromise between these three again compounds problems, and adds to these contradictions: since (one can now go on to say) replete positivity does not need the supplement of community in time, or of neutral reason, while tradition cannot admit a positive foundation that would render it redundant.

To overcome this hydra of an impasse, we need to understand from the work of many historians and theologians that Scripture, tradition and reason were simply *not* seen as separate sources prior to 1300. Throughout these considerations, the question will arise, first of all, should we want simply to *return* to this earlier perspective, or must we return with difference, given a certain validity to some of the newer post-1300 considerations? Second, how do we handle a situation in which there is a real secular sphere, as there was not in the Middle Ages? Can a certain earlier pre-1300 fluidity between faith and reason still help us out in our modern predicament?

The transformation of theology from the pre-1300 situation to the modern one will now be considered under three headings: the supernatural, the *corpus mysticum* and allegory. Through all these headings runs a fourth, which will not be explicitly considered on its own: this is participation. The first three categories derive mostly from the work of Henri de Lubac, especially as reinterpreted by Michel de Certeau, Jean-Yves Lacoste and Olivier Boulnois. The fourth category derives in part from Erich Przywara, Sergei Bulgakov, Hans urs von Balthasar and, again, Olivier Boulnois.

What is at issue under the first heading is theology between faith and reason; under the second, theology under ecclesial authority; under the third, theology between scripture and tradition.

II

It is a correct Catholic view, proclaimed since the time of the Church under persecution, that truth should be freely pursued, since all knowledge points towards God. Coercion into understanding defeats its own object, since the divine truth freely shines out everywhere. There is no question, then, but that the Church is in principle on the side of free scientific enquiry.

Since at least the Counter-Reformation however, the Catholic Church has tended to construe its support of science in terms of a duality of the realms of reason and faith. In the thought of Cardinal Cajetan, the Thomistic paradox of a natural desire for the supernatural, a desire that must be already the lure of grace, since humanity cannot raise itself to God of its own accord, is lost sight of.[3] Instead, Cajetan underwrites the late mediaeval and un-Thomistic espousal of a purely 'natural beatitude' accessible by philosophy, according to which the latter is supposed to be able to attain by natural powers of intellect and will to some sort of positive knowledge and contemplation of the divine.

By comparison, Aquinas had spoken of a philosophic reach to a negatively defined first cause, and in other statements indicated that even this reach is inseparable from a divine drawing forth by grace that defines humanity as such.[4] Cajetan instead espoused in effect a 'closed humanism' with its own transcendental reach, which was essentially unrelated to the arrival of revelation. Since there was no longer any natural anticipation of grace, faith was now construed in very 'extrinsicist' terms as assent to a series of revealed propositions; gradually, in a process culminating in Suarez, the notion of revelation also lost its integration of inner experience with interpretation of outward sign, and was bifurcated between one or the other.[5] The realm of grace now concerned external positive data superadded to the conclusions of reason, or else an ineffable realm of inner 'mystical' experience, equally positive and equally subject to experimental testing for reality of 'presence'.

As both Lacoste and Boulnois argue, modern 'philosophy' does not simply emancipate itself from theology – rather, it arises in a space that theology itself has carved out for it: the space of pure nature. To be sure, 'natural beatitude' was supposed to correspond roughly to the pagan *theoria* achieved by Plato and Aristotle. But this was a delusion: pagan *physis* was not Christian *natura*, since the latter exists only in paired contrast with the supernatural. It would be truer to say that the Platonic and Peripatetic philosophies contain some rough anticipation of the Christian supernatural, as much as they do of the Christian natural. For they both understand wisdom to be primarily the prerogative of the divine, and human wisdom as some degree of sharing in this replete wisdom.

Olivier Boulnois correctly radicalizes de Lubac's reading of Aquinas to show that the paradox of natural orientation to the supernatural in Aquinas is in fact in continuity with an entire cosmology and ontology which takes up themes from the Graeco-Arabic legacy, even though it transforms them in terms of a much stronger grasp of the idea of divine creation. Thus it is not simply that, as natural, we desire the supernatural, it is also that *intellect* as such, on the model of the angelic intellect that moves the celestial spheres, drawn in ceaseless perfect motion by the immoveable, only exists in the space of this paradox. Indeed, while all finite motions are proper to specific natures, nature as a whole is only in motion because drawn beyond herself by higher powers towards a stilling of motion. The motion of human intellect is like a more intense and reflexive influx and concentration of natural motion as such, while the celestial spheres combine the inwardness of the intellect of the separate substances that move them with the totality of circulating finite motion.

In this way, the natural human destiny towards the vision of God is only the outworking in a conscious, knowing and willing created nature of the paradox of creation as such: it is of itself nothing, and only exists by participation. (Creation for this reason requires a *purer* sense of *methexis*, as grasped by the Biblical teaching of the presence of wisdom and glory in the cosmos; thus St Paul with self-conscious irony proclaimed *methexis* to the Athenians: 'God in whom we live and move and have our being.') Therefore everything, not just humanity, is already as itself more than itself, and this more is in some sense a portion of divinity. It is not that something 'more' is added to the natural human soul – it is rather that the psychic is the conscious concentration of the paradoxical nature of every *ens* as such. Here, even though Aquinas rejects the Arabic doctrines of a single superhuman active intellect, he still nevertheless takes over their concern to attend to the phenomenology of thinking, which notes that we are never in charge of thought: thought occurs to us, and so thinking is certainly something thinking in us, as well as something that we think.

The collapse of the paradox of the natural orientation to the supernatural was an aspect of the collapse of this entire cosmology and ontology. Aquinas had sought a cause for finite being, *esse commune*, as such. But in the later Middle Ages, beginning, ironically, with Siger of Brabant, this was deemed a question that made little sense, since *esse* was no longer thought of as something superadded to essence, a notion which rendered an arriving accident paradoxically more fundamental than the essential itself in the constitution of the creature.[6] Instead, one could now only ask for the final cause of finite being in its given finite circumstances. But something finite *as existing* – the dog in its existing dogness, rather than the why of there being a dog, for example – was now regarded as making full sense in its own finite terms. In this way, to know that a being or a truth was from God was no longer held, as it was for Aquinas, to change the very character of the being or truth that was known. This new space of univocal existence, of sheer 'thereness', quickly became as much thereness for mere entertained thought as for ontic reality. Indeed the emergence of this space was itself inversely encouraged by a parallel drift, ever since Roger Bacon, away from the Aristotelian view that knowledge is the realization of migrating species as pure form in our mind, towards knowledge as representational mirroring of a reality having in itself no essential orientation toward understanding. Ideas and fictions now started to acquire ontological equality with real being as all equally 'things'.[7]

The new univocalist/representational space was the space that could be explored as the realm of pure nature. It extended beyond the finite: indeed, as Boulnois points out, Duns Scotus found it contradictory that Aquinas had combined the view that the primary object of the human intellect is sensory with the view that every act of understanding is oriented towards the supernatural.[8] Instead of Thomas' aporias and conundra, he substituted the view that the human intellect in its pure pre-lapsarian essence is naturally capable of the grasp of non-material essences: this (already, one wants to say 'transcendentalist' *à la* Rahner) reach of our intellect is then the natural base for the reception of positive supernatural information.

The combination of a univocalist and representational conception of understanding – our intellect represents 'things' which are simply there in their differential exemplifying of a bare 'presence' outside participation – with the idea of a natural beatitude permitted theology to encourage the emergence of independent philosophy faculties in the early modern period (the diverse presence of philosophy in mediaeval arts and theology faculties represented a totally different intellectual economy). There were now professional 'philosophers', where previously philosophy had survived as a kind of pagan 'moment' within Christian theology, which was linked with the necessary discursiveness of our finitude. Ironically, the new division of powers had itself in part emerged to counter the threat of Latin Averroism, which was thought (probably erroneously) to pursue a philosophy altogether independent of theology. The only drastic way to achieve institutional control over such tendencies was to purge theology itself of an essential metaphysical detour through a vision of the participatory reflection of the divine essence in the cosmos, and to insist that it is rather a purely positive discourse founded upon the divine *potentia absoluta*, now regarded as a real unknown reserve of limitless options. In this way there can be a final court of appeal against wayward reason, a court whose procedures are guaranteed, not so much by partial illuminatory intuition and dialectical discursiveness, but rather by recourse to positive sources and to methods for discriminating amongst and ordering those sources. This new positive approach was only really perfected in the sixteenth century, with the new insistence on theological loci, especially in the work of Melchior Cano.

What is important to grasp here is the to us counter-intuitive link between a new autonomy for philosophy and yet at the same time an increased censoring (or else aspiration to censor) philosophy by theology. This, I think, remains crucial for understanding our situation even today. But, as Jean-Yves Lacoste has well described, this had well-nigh ludicrous consequences: granted autonomy to explore pure nature, philosophers quickly did not find what they were supposed to find: soon they were announcing materialisms, pantheisms, idealisms and so forth; a little later they were disconnecting natural beatitude from any contemplation of the divine whatsoever. This meant that theologians did the only 'true' philosophy with their left hand. Philosophy was supposed to be able to reach natural truth solely by reason; however, as faith knew that the higher truth of revelation overrides apparently sound reasonings, every philosophy conflicting with faith must be denied twice over: once on positive grounds of faith, secondly in terms of a better reasoning which then has to be sought out.

Such convolutions surely have helped to bring Christianity into disrepute: yet they are entirely remote from the real outlook of the high Middle Ages. What is more, the 'bad' philosophers of modernity have always been more truly theological than the 'sound' ones. For they have refused to conclude God from uninflected objective reason, and thereby have inadvertently, and in some measure, avoided idolatry: all this has been set out in excellent detail, though from very different if complementary perspectives, by Michael Buckley and Jean-Luc Marion.[9]

But what we must now ask ourselves is whether or not the same mistakes are still being perpetuated today. For a long time now I have contended that Roman Catholic intellectual culture finds it very difficult, for institutional reasons, altogether to negate a false Tridentine legacy, and to pursue all the consequences of de Lubac's theological revolution (a subversion as real as it was stealthy). An enterprise of 'natural theology', which historians have now shown to go back at the very furthest only to Scotus, is perpetuated, along with a parallel discourse of 'natural law' considered in an un-Thomistic way, apart from the law of charity. This perpetuation is common to both 'conservatives' and 'liberals' – indeed, it is that secret common ground upon which they are distributed *as* conservatives and liberals, stressing respectively either faith or reason, but both assuming a two-tier economy. Even someone as influenced by de Lubac as Hans Urs von Balthasar, still pursues, unlike the former, a 'metaphysical' prolegomenon to *sacra doctrina*. When discussing Heidegger, he falls into exactly the same trap as Gilson: Heidegger has recovered the ontological difference already known to Thomas, yet does not 'pursue questioning far enough' by leaving the non-necessity of the ontic, and the excess of the ontological shown through this contingency, as a pure mystery. Further questioning is supposed to give rise ineluctably to the thought of Being as a personal donor.[10] But of course it does not: such a recourse remains also a 'mystery'; while Heidegger has after all his own resolution of the mystery: Being is also nothing; it is the continual presencing of absence in time.

In purely rational terms, Heidegger appears the more rigorous of the two, if by 'rational' one is speaking of the exploration of pure given nature as representable by our finite intellect and subject to the manoeuvrings of our finite will. As Jean-Yves Lacoste contends, the space of pure nature must confine the human essence to what the human being is itself on its own capable of, and must equally confine true human understanding to this capacity in its cognitive aspect.[11] Within such a confinement, we may add, our world will be defined by technological capacity, by an empty reach towards a sublime unknown and by systematic indeterminacy, since limits turn out to be themselves the perpetual anarchic transgression of limits (the inevitable post-modern turn of modernity), as well as by the horizon of death. As Lacoste points out, even the later Heidegger's exceeding of these options in terms of a symbolic dwelling within the cosmos remains a resignation to the impersonal, without hope beyond death, and so in subordination of the desires and aspirations of the body.

It would seem, then, that the history of modern ideas negatively bears out the view that no natural beatitude will be concluded towards, save under the promptings of an explicit orientation to the supernatural. This situation is half-recognized in the papal encyclical, *Fides et Ratio*.[12] There philosophy is exhorted to be 'wisdom' rather than merely 'reason', and this means to take account of right desiring, of the link between thought and life and to be open to receive something beyond the grasp of reason. This is all well and good, but needs further defining. The 'autonomy' of rational enquiry is still advocated, and not merely in terms of legal freedom (which one should of course endorse, in keeping with the early Christian view that truth can only be freely consented to) but also in terms of some essential good proceeding from such autonomy. However, if right desiring and openness to revelation have entered the picture, then, according to the post-de Lubac logic, this is already a work of grace, and already exists in some sort of typological, which is to say real historical, relation to scripture and tradition. What I mean by this is that all the traces of 'wisdom' on which philosophy might build in our modern world do not stand simply 'outside' Christian tradition, as far as this tradition is concerned. All ethical topics, for example, are marked by the passage of the Gospel through the world, and even when philosophy appeals to the Greeks, it appeals to a legacy that is taken up, in part, and in places, within the New Testament itself and thereby is now a constituent element of Christianity.

However, the exaggerated and somewhat naïve opposition of the encyclical to 'relativism', which militates against attention to historicity, means that the pursuit of wisdom cannot really be taken in this fashion. Instead, *Fides et Ratio* seems at times to insist upon a reason that is the same in all times and places, and is an autonomous natural faculty without presuppositions. In that case we are back with all the old post-Tridentine absurdities: the world is granted leave to think autonomously, yet left to itself it turns out that it cannot do this. So the Church ends up teaching the contradiction that autonomy needs assistance.

In the face of this situation, one natural reaction is a fideistic one. This reaction tells a story: once upon a time, it seemed as if the Church could rely upon metaphysical cosmology; then it seemed as if it could rely upon a metaphysical ethics, but now it must learn to cling to the Cross alone – perhaps construing even this as the tragic presence of God in his secular absence. It is the story told by Bonhoeffer, and also the story told in large measure by von Balthasar, especially in *Love Alone: The Way of Revelation*, although Balthasar still adds to revelation the (essentially Kantian, in the end) props of a phenomenological aesthetic and personalistic ethics taken as prolegomena, if admittedly only in part.[13] My noting this must make it sound as if I favour a Barthian critique of von Balthasar, and a purely fideistic recourse. But such is not in any way the case.

The profundity of the fideistic grand narrative turns out to be adolescent in character. What has been outgrown is not a natural childhood, but a non-innocent childhood of error which need never have happened – which is not *at all* to say that we should have remained forever in the culture of the twelfth and thirteenth centuries; no, it is an *unknown* future that we have missed and must seek to rejoin. Historical researches done since the 1960s make it abundantly clear that the metaphysical cosmology of the high Middle Ages was thoroughly informed by and transformed through the biblical legacy. When this metaphysics was lost, with the nominalists, it was not on the basis of a rediscovery of a biblical God of will, law and covenant and so on, but rather as the consequence of a catastrophic invasion of the West by ultimately Islamic norms (norms which we now turn back upon Islam, imagining them to be the 'other'). The very condemnations of 1277 by the Archbishops of Paris and

Canterbury which swept away a cultural legacy shared with Islam (as with Judaism and Byzantium) also repeated within the West a gesture of Islamic orthodoxy: banish and regulate philosophy; impose instead a positivistic order based upon literal punctilear revelation underwritten by absolute sovereignty, which is now the only trace on earth of an inscrutable deity. This is the 'Caliphization' of the West; the Bible now read as if it were the Koran; Calvin's *asharia* looming up on the horizon.

In the light of these developments, it proved in fact extremely difficult to think through the central Christian doctrines that depend upon realism of universals, reality of relation and the truth of *methexis* – all denied by the terminists. In consequence, Ockham's Trinity becomes three ontic persons within one unity of an individual; his Christology appears monophysite because he cannot think the divine hypostasis relationally; transubstantiation is trivialized into bilocation and extrinsicist miracle, and the Creation starts to acquire such autonomy that for Ockham there is no longer any 'reason' to ascribe its origin to God rather than to the intelligences. In consequence, all these doctrines become lifeless things no longer informing reason, and are rather matters merely to be believed on pain of death in this world or the next. They are now left to the Church as a huge pile of nakedly ideological resources.

So the cosmos of participation was never 'argued against' in some unanswerable fashion. There was simply an epistemic switch, complexly linked with social transformations, to representation and univocity. Certain tenets of natural philosophy may have been disproved, but even here one can exaggerate: Thomas Torrance has rightly pointed out how much nearer Robert Grosseteste's Christian/neo-Platonic cosmology of light, with its 'Cantorian' sets of nested differentiated infinites (and actually no celestial/terrestrial duality) was to modern physics than that of the later Middle Ages or of Newton.[14]

The point then is not at all that we must now cling to faith in ascetic nakedness. Instead, we must pass beyond the still all-too-modern fideism of neo-orthodoxy, towards a 'radical orthodoxy' that refuses the duality of reason over against faith. The issue is rather that what has recently passed for reason is not, as far as the Catholic faith is concerned, the work of the *logos* at all, or only jaggedly and intermittently so. Recent reason itself shows this, negatively, to be the case, since the strict rigorous upshot of its objective, representing regard is to discover the rule of unreason beyond reason, and the founding of sense in nonsense. Reason's domain is nihilism; whereas the discovery of a meaningful world governed by a *logos* can only be made by faith. This is perhaps the nearest one can get to an apologetic gesture (and I am echoing the thought of Jacobi), but it still does not decide the issue, ineluctably.

What has passed for reason is, as Lacoste suggests, a mere decision to see that which is Promethean-like within our capacity as the key to our nature and the key to unlock the secrets of the world, or else the key to a knowable world limited to the truth that arises for our purposes. This, of course, has often been seen as a pious gesture: confine reason and nature within their limits, thereby let the gratuity of grace in its glory all the more shine out upon us. Even in the case of Kant, a true reading shows that he is trying to protect a rarefied and anti-liturgical pietist faith from contamination by limited images, much more than he is trying to protect reason from contamination by religion – Kant, the last Scotist, Ockhamist, Suarezian, as he has been variously described. The Kantian attempt to acknowledge limits self-deconstructs, since limits will only appear if one claims absolutely to surmount them, and thus one gets Kant's after all dogmatic hierarchy of practically perceived noumena above theoretically perceived phenomena. Yet even a post-modern, deconstructed Kant, wherein the sublime overflows every temporary restraint, still erects a shrine to pure nature and the confines of reason: its mark is now the hypostatization of the unknown as only an empty void, and refusal of any possibility of 'beautiful' mediation between the invisible and the visible.

However, this worship of limits that constructs pure reason is only a *decision*, without reasons. As Lacoste has best explained, such a decision adopts a hermeneutic of the human essence and of nature, which makes that which lies within perceived capacity fundamental. But supposing the human aspiration to, or even openness to, that which lies beyond its capacity, were taken as the hermeneutic key instead? Lacoste here puts in a sharper light the insistence of many modern Christians – Charles Péguy supremely – upon the virtue of hope. Reason oriented only to a beatitude supposedly within its grasp dispenses with the virtue of hope, only to land up as without the sentiment of hope, and at best resigned to this condition. Likewise, if such a reason is taken as hermeneutically decisive, it must downgrade the promptings, urgings and longings of the body. The supernatural in us may be intelligence as such, intelligence thinking through us, but it is also always conjoined with sensation, as Aquinas taught. Therefore intelligence begins as a bodily exercise, accompanied by desire that reaches into the unknown. Only by the exercise of an artificial abstraction can we prise reason apart from desire, which reaches beyond our capacity. This prised-apart 'pure reason' is also a totally individualistic reason, whether on the level of the single person or of collective humanity. For such a *logos*, I cannot be completed by the other, and so others cannot mediate to me the lure of a 'wholly Other' who is also 'not other' as *intimo interior meo*, according to the creationist logic of paradoxical priority of supplementation.

What *faith* proposes as *reason*, then, is taking as hermeneutic keys to reality, first, *hope*, and then *charity* which is the erotic lure of the other and our giving ourselves over to the other. How does such a perspective affect the task of theology today? Primarily, it absolutely forbids us to baptize the secular desert as the realm of pure reason, pure nature, natural law or natural rights and so forth. For this is not at all to acknowledge this sphere in its integrity, but instead it is to define it in terms of an impoverished baroque theology, even though it still defines itself in this way, as if everyone were really a headless theologian. Rather what is truly current today is a post-modern simultaneity of remote times, places and cultures. It cannot be dealt with in terms of a single Western liberal narrative of pure nature, because this will only issue in bombs and destruction of the other. And none of this complex confusion is exactly 'outside' the Church. The Church reads it all in terms of multiple but converging narratives of typological anticipation, unrecognized scattering of the seeds sown by the incarnate *Logos*, and various fallings-away and partial survivals of Christian norms.

So the answer cannot be the Tracy one: responsibility before a uniform liberal court. This court itself is a fiction, and one moreover whose dark inner secret is constitution by a voluntarist theology securing order through the formal regulation of chaos from a single sovereign centre. Such a liberal option in theology in fact remains confined within a logic constructed by extrinsicism. Its essentially authoritarian character is revealed when it stamps philosophical conclusions already arrived at with a theological seal of approval derived from doctrines that extrinsically symbolize supposedly universal truths.

But nor can the answer be a fideistic one. And it cannot even be the Ratzinger one, to the extent that this is not entirely self-consistent, and still preserves, like von Balthasar, traces of a metaphysical prolegomenon, even for Christians, and of a somewhat still too positivistic account of revealed truth. Revelation is not in any sense a layer added to reason. It arrives as the augmentation of illumination, and faith is found only in the highly complex and tortuous course of a reason that is hopeful and charitable. It is lodged in all the complex networks of human practices, and its boundaries are as messy as those of the Church itself. Henri de Lubac's paradox forbids us to privilege either a human above or a human below. Rather, what has real priority in his scheme is the supernatural, which so exceeds our human hierarchies that it includes every degree of them in equality and is as near to the below as to the above. So although the lure of the supernatural takes precedence over nature that is drawn towards it (and this cannot be perverted into the transcendentalist terms of Rahner), this lure is only acknowledged by aspiring nature in all her lowly variety. Theological truth first of all abides in the body of the faithful. Yet where are their various bodies, especially today? Not neatly gathered in, that is for sure. Rather disseminated outwards into complex mingling and associations. A faith obedient to the Church is protected from solipsism precisely at the point where one recognizes that the Church always has been, as John Henry Newman recognized, itself the taking up and intermingling of many human traditions. It even consists from the outset in a seeing how the diverse might cohere, and continues to enact this analogical fusion.

Therefore I do not find the plural space of the academy, as perhaps *best* symbolized by religious studies departments, wherein alone *alternative* traditions of reason are sometimes recognized, to be totally other to the space of the Church that is also pluralistic and also construes its truth, as does the Bible, to be in one of its aspects a certain narration of 'the history of religions'. The difference is that the Church has a project of integration, to which the theologian is bound. Within both the academy and the Church, the task of theology is to foreground the Christian difference and non-difference – to think through the Christian *logos* as something entirely exceptional, which also continues and elevates what is most usual to humanity.

How exactly, though, does theology relate to Church authority? This is the question we must turn to next, under the heading, *corpus mysticum.*

III

How are we to understand the nature of ecclesial authority and its bearing upon theology? Jean-Luc Marion has said in *Dieu Sans L'Etre* that the key is to realize that the bishop is the true theologian.[15] I think that he is precisely right, but that his point has usually been misunderstood (especially in the United States). What he is invoking of course, is a vital link between theology and the Eucharist. The bishop is the original president at the Eucharist; he is also the prime preacher of the word, a function that he performs only in conjunction with his re-presenting of the body and blood of Christ. The idea that all theologians must sub-derive their authority as theologians from the bishop, is only authoritarian under an erroneous understanding of the relationship of the bishop to the Eucharist, to the word of God and to his *cathedra*, which is at once his teaching office and also literally the place where he sits and presides, usually a city of long standing.

However, such an erroneous understanding was already encouraged by shifts in the conception of the Church and its relation to the Eucharist in the late mediaeval and early modern period. As de Lubac described these transformations, the term *corpus verum* ceased, roughly after the mid-twelfth century, to be applied to the Church, and was transferred to the body of Christ in the Eucharist. Inversely, the term *corpus mysticum* migrated from the Eucharist to the Church.[16] Gradually, the latter was drained of physical solidity, which was transferred to the transubstantiated elements. 'Mystical' slowly ceased to mean 'to do with the liturgical mysteries of initiatory passage, participation and ascent' and came to denote secrecy, absence and symbolism. Accompanying this transformation was a change in the relation of both bodies to the historical body of Christ. Earlier, the sacramental and ecclesial bodies stood near each other, and both re-presented the historical body. But in the new scheme, the historical and sacramental bodies start to stand near each other as alien sources of authority over against the Church, which, as Michel de Certeau stresses in his brilliant commentary on de Lubac's *Corpus Mysticum* and *Exegese Medievale*, increasingly comes to be seen as an ideal space to be constructed in order to realize the dicta of authority, or else to make manifest a new inner 'mystical' experience which is the residue of liturgical ascent that finds no place in a more legal and less liturgical construal of the public sphere.[17]

As long as an essential relation between the three bodies remained, however, strong traces of the older view persisted – for example, in the thought of Bonaventure or of Thomas Aquinas. It remained the case that the historical body was mediated to the Church by the sacramental body. The Eucharist still 'gave' the Church, in such a fashion that, as Catherine Pickstock puts it, the Church was not a closed self-governing entity like most political bodies (whether hierarchic or democratic), but rather received its very social embodiment from outside itself.[18] At every Eucharist it had, as it were, to begin again, to receive itself anew from outside, from the past and from the angelic Church above. Inversely, the transubstantiation of the bread and wine into the body and blood of Christ was seen as a dynamic action of divine self-giving inseparable from the bringing about and consolidating of the body of the faithful. (Incidentally, the term 'transubstantiation' is much older than the term 'real presence' which perhaps originates with Latimer and Cranmer – *praesentia corporalis* was used in the Middle Ages but shied away from by Aquinas – and is dubiously linked with a static sense of local presence that is also 'over against' the congregation.)[19]

The really drastic change came when, as de Certeau following de Lubac stresses, the sacramental body ceased to operate this mediating function. Then, instead of a triad one had alternating dyads: a direct relation of either the absent historical body as testified to by scripture to the Church, or else of the sacramental body to the Church, now taken as a source of authority *independent* of Scripture and rather deriving from a hierarchic transmission of ecclesial orders. As de Certeau concludes, this eventually brings about a total shift from a priority of the diachronic to a priority of the synchronic and functional. Previously, the past had really been made present again through the Eucharist and the Church had re-emerged through its sustaining of a bond to the past and projection forwards to the future, by re-offering of the sacraments and reinterpretation of the *sacra Scriptura*. Now, instead, the past started to seem like a remote lost source of authority which historical detective work must flush out (thus the rise of humanist concern with 'historicity'). As remote, it stood apart from and over against the Church, which no longer re-presented it. Its relationship to the other sacramental source of authority was bound now to be disputed, since the sacramental body was no longer seen as an essential way in which the lost historical body as traced out by the scriptures was 'performed' again in the present. Either sacraments as validated by tradition were seen as an essential supplement to the now remote scriptures, as in the late mediaeval and Tridentine views, or else the need for this supplement was rejected, and one was left with the Protestant *sola Scriptura*. But de Certeau's drastic conclusion here is both rigorous and undeniable: the crucial shift was certainly not the Reformation – rather, Protestantism and Tridentine Catholicism represented two alternative versions of 'reformation' which should be defined as the switch from the triadic to the dyadic account of the relation of the various bodies of Christ. It is this sort of realization that could be the ground for a more honest and self-critical ecumenism.

Under the new perspective, the power of clerical authority was necessarily increased. For when the historical body was again made present in the Eucharist, and the eucharistic body was only fully realized in the congregation, primary authority was both symbolic and collective, and initially bypassed vertical hierarchy. Only by a sort of reflex was Episcopal authority constituted. The bishop was first of all powerful as identified with a particular *cathedra* which was a specific intersection of time and place that recorded a particular Christian fulfilment of a particular local legacy: thus nearly all churches were built on earlier sacred sites, and this was not at all primarily a matter of propaganda, but of vital continuity in and through a surpassing. As president at the Eucharist and teacher from his chair, the Bishop enacted once again the essence of a certain place (usually the abode of sacred relics) and perpetuated the stream of glory refracted through it in a specific way. The bishop held authority, from Ignatius of Antioch onwards, as symbolizing in his singleness the unity of the Church in a single *civitas*.

Of course the bishop was also the guardian and guarantor of correct transmission, and of course his exercise of these powers might often in reality overstep the mark of his representational and dramatic function: nevertheless, it remained the case up to the mid-thirteenth century or so that clerical sacramental and preaching authority was much more 'mingled' with lay participation than it later became, although at first in the later Middle Ages the laity defended itself with the increased activity of semi-independent lay fraternities.[20] But during this period the techniques of remote, secret and invasive clerical control as deployed through auricular confession, exorcism and staged miracles, first mooted in the twelfth century and promulgated through the Lateran Councils, were vastly extended. The 'gothic' realm of complex overlapping spaces and social participations started to give way to the 'gothick' realm of systematic terror through *surveillance*; it is no accident that one of the great 'gothick' novels of the eighteenth century, the Irish protestant Charles Maturin's *Melmoth the Wanderer*, deploys a critique of the Spanish Inquisition also as a critique of Calvinist predestinationism and of modernity as such.[21]

This increased clerical control was inseparable from the new economy of the three bodies. For no longer was the transmission of authority carried through in a superhuman 'angelic' fashion by the liturgical action. No longer did the historical body pass via the Bishop into the mouths of communicants or (more often) the eyes of witnesses, who then 'performed' what the liturgical script suggested. Instead, the historical and sacramental bodies were now more like inert objects in need of human subjective assistance. For the magisterial Reformation, the ordained clergy were the privileged interpreters of the word, who quickly established 'orthodox' parameters within which it could be read, so neutralizing its supposedly self-interpreting authority, as Catholic critics swiftly pointed out. For Tridentine Catholicism, the ordained hierarchy was the guarantee of a Eucharistic miracle now seen as a spectacle quite apart from its dynamic action of 'giving' the body of the Church.

So we cannot possibly talk of an increased lay influence in Protestantism over against a Catholic clericalist reaction. Rather, in either case there is a substantial loss of mediaeval lay participation (as the British Catholic historians, John Bossy, John Scarisbrick and Eamon Duffy have all argued),[22] while in either case there is also a significant rise in compensating lay pieties and mysticisms which try to colonize the no-man's-land which had now arisen in the gap between a closed humanism on the one hand, and an extrinsicist system of dogma on the other. As de Certeau argues, a 'mystic' discourse arises with a redoubling of the sense of the absence of a true ecclesial body, although it is often itself recruited into the machinations of ecclesiastical discipline and the attempts to verify abstractions with experience and build a new future on the basis of formal method.

It would seem, then, that the earlier, high mediaeval model offers us a much better understanding of the relation of the Bishop to teaching and so to theological reflection. Theology is answerable to the Bishop as the occupant of the *cathedra* and as president at the Eucharist. But this means that the theologian is primarily answerable, not so much to a Church hierarchy in its synchronic spatiality – this is all too modern – but rather to a hierarchical, educative *manuductio* of the faith down the ages. Equally, he is answerable to a specific locality or, very often, multiple specific localities, such that his sense of perpetuating a history must be combined with his sense of carrying out an archaeology and mapping a geography. Finally, he is also answerable to the mode of the reception of sacrament and word by the congregation, even if this now in this century is often impossible and the theologian must exercise what is an excessively critical function by ideal standards.

But this sounds all rather abstract. Who really constrains the theologian and to what degree? The Bishop? The Congregation? And how are we to understand the workings of ecclesiastical hierarchy today in the realm of knowledge, given the great approval that the Church appears to give to democracy in the secular sphere?

IV

To try to answer these questions somewhat, I want to invoke the thought of Nicholas of Cusa in his early work, the *De Concordantia Catholica*.[23] Despite this being a conciliarist treatise, Nicholas' later papalist position did not abandon its essential conclusions. It is very interesting from our point of view, because it almost uniquely preserves at a very late date a much earlier perspective upon the mediating role of sacramental signs between the historical and ecclesial bodies. At the same time, it shows traces also of more modern elements that are perhaps of a kind that are inescapable today: a new stress upon mass assembled participation in the present, and upon historical variation that is due to the cultural variety of human imaginings. In addition, Nicholas, following Augustine and other patristic sources, anticipates an apocalyptic time when the Church will be in terminal decline: which may be our situation today. So perhaps Nicholas provides some keys not merely to recovering the lost pre-1300 world, but also to going forward now to the future we might always have had, yet never yet have had.

Cusanus sustains the thesis that the Eucharist gives the Church. For him what stands topmost in the Church hierarchy is not a *de jure* legal power, but rather sacramental signs. In this way, in the tradition of Dionysius, the ecclesial and the experiential are still fused through the liturgical mysteries. The sacramental signs for Nicholas correspond at a lower level of the cosmic hierarchy to the Triune God at the very top of the hierarchy. God is said fully to know the members of the Church in love, and they are oriented to the Trinity through a desire that exceeds their intellection – a very Eastern element here. (Nicholas was of course centrally involved in the attempts to reunite Eastern and Western Christendom that culminated in the Council of Constance.) This desire is mediated to us through the operation of all the sacraments.

The next rank within the heavenly *ecclesia*, eternal Jerusalem (wherein God 'is' through all perpetuity, as in later Russian sophiology) below God, is the angelic. The angels, in a rather Arabic fashion, see into all human intellects, and human thought especially puts us into contact with the separate intelligences. Within the ecclesial hierarchy, the priesthood is linked to the angelic in terms of its teaching function, and its occupancy of *cathedrae*, since the *Apocalypse* tells us that angels are guardians of ecclesial places.

In the third rank come the blessed in heaven who link to humanity on earth through the body, and who correspond to the body of the faithful within the Church militant here below.

There are certain complications within this scheme: the clergy in relation to their *orders* correspond to the first sacramental rank, but this seals the priority of their sacramental, transmissive function over their authoritative, teaching one. In fact the clergy span all three degrees because, in terms of their participation with the laity in intercessory offices, they belong to the lowest level that simply praises and does not mediate between lower and higher levels. In addition, there seems to be a certain lack of consistency: the laity are the most bodily, and yet their function of praise is also a spiritual synthesis of sacramental sign and physically situated *cathedra*. The same lack of clarity pertains in the heavenly church: the resurrected faithful are the most corporeal and yet their third psychic position (in keeping with the neo-Platonic hierarchy of the One, *nous* and *psyche*) also synthesizes through desire the Origin that is God and the expressed (so imaged) intellection that belongs to the angels. The confusion perhaps has its source in the blending of Proclus with Trinitarian theology. For all these degrees also correspond for Nicholas to the respective persons of the Trinity, and though the Son as *logos* is intellectual, as *imago* he is also somewhat 'corporeal', compared with the unity in desire shown by the Spirit.

It is in fact the presence of the Trinity at the top of the hierarchy that has a deconstructive effect at every level of the hierarchy; although Nicholas also inherits the deconstructions inherent in Proclean neo-Platonism itself. But he offers in this treatise the fullest exhibition ever of the multiple paradoxes of hierarchy: indeed, out of them he generates an early democratic theory. The idea that he simply 'mixes' mediaeval hierarchy with proto-modern democracy is simply not the case: instead, he returns to earlier high mediaeval mystical and educative notions of hierarchy, and out of these notions themselves generates new democratic theses. This gives a basis for conciliarism and consensus quite other to the contractualist one of William of Ockham, which blasphemously reduces Church government to a balance of power between formally considered individual forces.

Let us begin with the paradoxes already glimpsed by neo-Platonism. Paradox one: a hierarchy, to be a hierarchy, requires stages, else it would be a quality-less flux. But then a stage can only be distinguished within a flux if it marks out a *level*, which will be a field of equality. To sustain the ontological primacy of hierarchy – every emanation from on high is continuously diminishing – the level must itself be broken up as a hierarchy within a hierarchy, and of course this threatens a *mise en abyme*, indicated in Cusa's text by a slightly insane process of triadic sub-dividing on the part of an author who of course knew that finitude itself was subject to infinite division. A consequence of this logic of levels is that the subordinate within a certain stage is nonetheless equal, with its subordinateness entirely cancelled, to all members of that stage, if one rises to a more fundamental hierarchical viewpoint.

It is just this that provides Nicholas with his fundamental conciliarist principle. From the *highest* perspective, all that is created is on a level; within the Church militant all its members are on a level, just as the sacramental and ecclesial bodies are on a level. Since the true ontological character of the Church, following Augustine, is peace and harmony, which for Cusa is extended into *discors concordia*, the first ruling principle within the Church is consensus. Not of course in the first place majority rule, but absolute consensus. For the Church is not first and foremost a vehicle of correct teaching: it is rather first and foremost the *event* of *concordantia*. Doctrine is about nothing but the giving of divine *concordantia* in the Creation and its restoration through the Incarnation and the Church. Hence there cannot be true teaching without consensus, even if, one might add, this consensus and the key to harmony can dwindle to being present only in a few, as Augustine anticipates will eventually happen when there will be left only the 'last of the last'.[24] It is for this reason that teaching is inseparable from the guarantee of the Holy Spirit's presence in the Church: in the long run and for the most part, the members of the Church will be reliable, because without this there could *be* no true doctrine. For doctrine is first of all a body and not simply words: Christ was the supreme teacher as the event of the return of *concordantia* to the world. For truth there must be democratic consent, although this must also be a uniting in 'the right way' according to the true measure of harmony. If 'democracy' failed, the Church would cease to be; however, the keys to democratic consensus must much of the time be safeguarded by an ecclesiastical elite, gathered round the bishops.

At this point the significance of the nested hierarchy within each level comes to the fore. It is not really a principle in opposition to 'democracy'. That is only the case, where, within a closed immanent circle based upon a balance of interests between forces, a sovereign centre is granted *de facto* power. This is why liberalism always generates terrifying hierarchies not linked to the transmission of values: hierarchies of money and bureaucratic organization and policing. Here one has the necessary authoritarian counterpart to the mitigated anarchy of market society. By contrast, the power that Nicholas invests in the *cathedra* is a salve against the closure that the emerging sovereign state and later liberal democracy would soon place around a specific, often 'national' community. In fact, even a global community is closed against a wider democracy if it is only 'in the present'. This is the point of Edmund Burke's appeal to the votes of all the ages. A similar principle in Nicholas supports the view that the Bishop and those gathered round him must especially sustain the *concordantia* with the past and preserve the resources of the past for the future against the likely ravages of the present. Thus the Bishop is poised between the always-arriving order of signs and the consensus of the people that can alone fulfil that order. His authority derives from both. But ultimately, of course, he must appeal to the widest democracy of all: the original *concordantia* of the whole cosmos, grounded in the consensus of the Trinity, which Cusa in this work already presents as the coincidence of the opposites of the one and the many.

Nicholas's ecclesiology results from the interplay between the democratic and aristocratic principles, combined with a monarchic one in terms of the papacy. But even in the latter case the stress is upon *cathedra*: the Pope's authority is that of an ancestral place.[25] A place that has been the focal intersection of so much for so long, evil as well as good, is likely to have a certain priority in terms of the persistence of the rhythms of the truth. This is the kind of way in which Cusanus puts things. The same applies to every Episcopal seat in a lesser degree. So in fact a single principle legitimates *both* the democratic and the aristocratic aspects. This principle is 'for the most part'. Applied synchronically, one gets democracy: the consensus of the entire laity and clergy is the most reliable guide – a Newman-like principle. Applied diachronically, one gets aristocracy: the longest persisting locations and their representatives will be the least likely to err. Yet the entire diachrony merges with an eternal synchrony: the voices of all times and places are the final court of appeal, insofar as these voices sing with one true voice of praise.

Thus infallibility, speaking *ex cathedra*, works in the following way for Cusanus. True infallibility resides in the whole Church on account of the hypostatic presence of the Holy Spirit, without which human salvation would be null and void. Then it resides in the conciliar assembly of the bishops, and finally in the supreme *cathedra* of Rome, the longest abiding seat of sacred legitimacy. The Pope is the supreme guardian: he has the right to summon a general council. But the consensus of the council is a more reliable locus of infallibility than the Pope, as in turn it is weaker than the entire *ecclesia*. A council has the right to depose a false Pope – and Nicholas even sustained this view in his later papalist phase.

But throughout these considerations, which owed much to Cyprian as well as to Augustine, Nicholas never lost sight of his sense of the primacy of the sacramental. This primacy, as Augustine saw against the Donatists, ensures that even erring clergy can be true ministers. For the belief in the infallibility of the Church is not a peculiar superstition: instead it resides finally in our trust in certain signs. Since we cannot command the meaning of any sign, true signs will always outwit our worst intentions, and inhabit us promisingly despite ourselves. This is how the Holy Spirit is hypostatically present in the Church.

A second paradox of hierarchy is that the higher element within a lower stage must always be more akin to the *lower* stages above itself than the higher stages above itself. This is aporetic, because stages involve not just a smooth descent but rather a regular folding back of the whole process upon itself to produce the instance of stages, such that the higher element within each stage reinvokes the summit *out of series*, while the lower element anticipates the nethermost base, also out of series. Neo-Platonism was fully aware that, to produce a distinct new level that must in a measure 'hold back' the free fall of emanation, a new charge from the original source must somehow flow down the chain and, to a degree, interrupt the process of diminution. Or to put this the other way around: a distinct new phase must somehow override the immediately higher intermediaries and reinvoke the origin directly.

For example, if the hierarchy runs throughout from Spirit to Body, the higher elements in lower stages will be more spiritual than the lower elements within that stage, but more bodily than everything higher up, in such a fashion that these elements shift undecidedly between 'more spiritual' and 'more bodily'. In consequence there will be an increasing tendency as one descends the hierarchy to perceive even the topmost dimensions of stages as 'more bodily', and thus an asymptotic tendency *to reverse* the hierarchy in the lower stages altogether. Ethnographers have discovered that many local tribes with symbolic hierarchies actually carry through this reversal, so that, for example, 'male' will be on top in a higher realm, and 'female' in a lower.

This second paradox tends to produce explicit reversal in the lower realm, and parallel orders of hierarchy, albeit hierarchically arranged. In the case of Cusanus, this happens with the body of the faithful. Insofar as they are more fleshly, then fleshly concerns here assume priority. The emperor, who in turn is within a separate hierarchy that owes direct responsibility to the Trinity, governs the laity of the Church.[26] The authenticity of the donation of Constantine is denied by Nicholas, and the crowning of the Emperor is seen as confirmation of an already proclaimed power, as applies also to the coronation of the Pope. Yet of course the realm of the emperor still belongs to *ecclesia*: Cusa, unlike his contemporaries, is still not yet talking about 'the State'. Concerns of the flesh remain ultimately subordinate to those of the spirit, and the Emperor like the Pope is still answerable to the infallibility of the entire body of the Church. Insofar as this is concentrated and focused in the Pope, he also remains in some sense answerable to Rome. Indeed, he is of course the Holy Roman Emperor. (Nicholas' perspective is naturally Germanic.)

A third paradox of hierarchy is much accentuated by Trinitarian theology. The origin of a hierarchy cannot merely be the highest rung: as the source of every stage it must transcend hierarchy as such and even equalize within itself all stages of the hierarchy, negating their differentiation. This is the neo-Platonic doctrine of the mystical One. However, the Trinity tends to turn this non-differentiation into preservation as much as obliteration of the many, as Nicholas stresses. But this increases the sense that at the top, degree is crossed out. Furthermore, as we have seen, hierarchy requires distinguished stages, and in fact a minimum of three stages, since if there were only two there would not be mediation and interval and therefore no stages at all. So Nicholas, like neo-Platonism in general, posits three main stages, and sub-divides his stages into three also. But the Trinity teaches that the One is also Three and therefore that it 'complicates' what hierarchy 'explicates', to use Cusan terminology. We have already seen that within every stage the totality of the stage ranks above the topmost rank within a stage, so that, for example, the Bishop is above the laity, but the whole Church is above the Bishop. The invocation of a Creator God, however, makes this principle apply more emphatically to the totality of everything. Since all differences of rank are utterly subordinated to the qualitatively different difference of rank between Creator and Created, the totality of the cosmos emphatically comes next after God, rather than the created intelligences. Moreover, because in the Triune God the second and the third stage are equal and co-original, this means that the paradox of levelling as one ascends the hierarchical ladder is much more carried over into the absolute itself which thereby much more validates cosmic levelling. In this levelling, the Trinity is itself manifest. Therefore at the summit of the created hierarchy all the lower degrees are now fully equalized: body is restored to parity with spirit, as occurs in the resurrection of the dead.

The cosmos one is concerned with here, however, is really the totality of the restored cosmos concentrated in the heavenly Jerusalem: the angels and the resurrected faithful with God in his glorious presence. The latter is the Sophia that is also the ground of the procession of the Son and the Spirit in the Trinity for modern Russian theology or the primal 'outgoing' that Gregory of Nyssa named *dynamis* and Dionysius in the plural *dynameis*. At this highest level then, one can infer, the laity and the Emperor are equalized with the Bishop, while the latter's *cathedra* is equalized with sacramental signs now fully realized. Indeed, via the resurrected body of the Lamb in the heart of the eternal city, the Bride Jerusalem is equalized with God and drawn through deification entirely into the life of the Trinity.

So the principle of hierarchical ascension guards truth against democracy, but the more ascension is enacted, the more also democracy is implemented in the truth. It is not that democracy is a compromise for here and now: it is that it can only finally arrive in the perfection of *concordantia* as deification. To eternalize democracy, and maintain its link with excellence rather than the mutual concessions of baseness, deification as the doctrine of the offer of equality with God is required.

Such divine democracy is approximated to here below in the processes of historical *traditio*. For Nicholas as a 'Renaissance' thinker, these now include a passage through the cultural relativity of different human fictioning: different sacraments and sacrifices in all human cultures, that nonetheless all really indicate the one sign of Christ and his sacrifice.[27] It is here that a 'modern' factor comes into the picture: a new sense that human institutions really do spring from collective 'makings'. Such a sense is also what pushes Cusa towards bringing out the latent democratic implications of an inherited and highly traditional (indeed in his day totally out-of-date) Trinitarian and liturgical hierarchical vision. Even hierarchical structures are erected by fashioned consensus, beginning with God himself. Truly Nicholas was 'radically orthodox'.

For Cusa, as for Augustine, the ontological diminution through emanation worked also downwards through time. For Augustine, the sixth age of the world inaugurated by Christ is human old age, marked by decline and a worsening of the effects of the Fall. Yet, here also, the paradoxes intrude, reinforced by Trinitarian theology: direct contact with the origin can be established even in senescence. At almost the end, there has been absolute rejuvenation: thus for Augustine 'progress' becomes possible for the first time in the era of ultimate degeneration. Here is an absolute duality: as W.H. Auden understood in his libretto for the Christmas Oratorio 'For the Time Being', the Incarnation institutes a time of dread when we have to live in the partial meaninglessness of an aftermath to the appearance of the ultimate – to live in absolute waiting for the consummation of what was begun and yet is 'for the time being' suspended. It is also the time of terrible demand for perfection in the body and therefore the time when this absolute demand for goodness will be rejected and, in Augustinian terms, evil in its nakedness as Antichrist will appear. For Augustine, the faithful in the face of this terror are likely to be few and will get fewer, until we reach the 'last of the last'. Nicholas agreed, and thought he had reached that period. He gave the world 600 more years (writing in the *De Concordantia* in 1433) until Europe had been destroyed and yet Christ preached throughout the world. Therefore he anticipated in a sense both globalization and the end of Christendom. Yet this disastrous era is also precisely the time for him in which a conciliar and democratic ideal that will truly reflect the Trinity can at last be achieved on earth. Disaster will make us see more truly.

It is in a sense comforting to realize that our predicament was from the outset foreseen, for Augustine and Nicholas only build upon Christ's warnings and promises in the gospels. Neither triumphalism nor celebration of secular autonomy is here suggested. Rather, there will be catastrophic refusal of charity. However, the hypostatic presence of the Holy Spirit on earth will not fail, and hence the 'time being' will still prove a time of meaningful realization of deified democracy: even especially in the further darkening period towards the end. There will be decline . . . and yet there will be progress.

V

Theology, therefore, is answerable to reason precisely insofar as it is answerable to the Church. And in the latter domain it is first of all answerable to the Triune God, since theology is a participation in the mind of God before it is obedience to any authority, whether scriptural or hierarchical. But as such it is equally a participation in the whole deified Church as the heavenly Jerusalem. The latter is only encountered through earthly mediation, and here theology is first answerable to the whole Church militant, but this involves a certain answerability to the Bishop in the way that we have seen.

But in what way is theology also answerable to Scripture? Here, once again, we can only see clearly when we refuse post-1300 dualities. As we saw, Protestantism privileged the historical body of Christ, Trent the sacramental body. Equally, this meant a preference either for Scripture or for tradition, respectively. But prior to Henry of Ghent, there had been no such juxtaposition. He for the first time asked which had priority, thereby revealing that something had already altered.[28] Now it seemed it was already the case that Scripture was a closed book in the past that needed supplementing by a separate oral command. Basil had spoken of written and unwritten traditions, but the latter were seen by him and by later theologians as consisting in the 'performance' of the text itself. *Traditio* was the handing over of the text into practice. Thus Thomas Aquinas speaks of *sacra Scriptura* as the sole authority for *sacra doctrina*, in a way that sounds 'Protestant' by later Tridentine standards. But he is not speaking of the Protestant Bible. There was, as yet, no single bound printed book, but many manuscripts of different books of the Bible, usually surrounded by patristic commentary. Gregory the Great had said that, when he read and commented on the Bible, the text itself expanded.[29] It was up to the commentator to go on trying to achieve the Bible as the infinite 'Borgesian' library spoken of at the end of St John's Gospel, as it was equally up to the painter and stager of miracle plays. Such a 'Novalis-like' or 'Mallarmean' perspective was also presupposed by the entire practice of allegorical exegesis. This rendered theology possible by showing how Christological and ecclesial restoration of the world depended upon the assumption of a divine 'rhetoric of things'. Things referred to in the Old Testament were already redeemed, since they pointed forwards allegorically to Christ: in the 'time being' after Christ, we could be redeemed, because his deeds indicated and made possible our anagogical performances. As de Certeau says, all this depended upon a sense that there were 'essential' shared universal meanings between things: in consequence nominalism ensured the collapse of allegory as the real divine rhetoric and so of the true inner basis of Christian theology. Without real intrinsic aesthetic connections, the ways of God in history became indecipherable, and one was left instead with a series of positive institutions, only linked as logically possible manifestations of the divine absolute power. Logical reflection upon this situation was now divorced from ontology, and the rhetorical dimension of scripture and preaching was from hence forwards somewhat confined to mere human words. The 'treatise on sacred rhetoric' emerged within both a Reformation and a counter-Reformation ambience.

It is nevertheless true that in various ways de Certeau exaggerates. Indeed, his own somewhat 'nihilistic' (in a strictly technical sense) theology seems to require the later decadent situation of bodily absence to be normative. He exaggerates the negativity of the 'time being'. The Church is not just, as he says, a mystical substitute for the lost real Israel and living body of Christ: it also truly is in all its physicality and placement in *cathedrae* still exactly both these things. It only lost this positivity through the processes traced by de Lubac and de Certeau himself. Moreover, are we to perceive the work of the univocalist/nominalist Antichrist within the Church only negatively? Without lapsing into Hegelian dialectic, one can acknowledge that catastrophe may help one to see more clearly, and that the nominalist critique exposes certain faults to view. There are three points to be made here.

First of all, in the face of nominalism and univocity, Nicholas of Cusa realized that both realism about universals, and analogical participation, require one to see the limited scope of the law of identity, for Ockham says with some truth that a common essence would be in the same respect both particular and universal and that an analogous *esse* would be in the same respect both shared and proper.[30] Nicholas sees that, outside finite limits, this law no longer holds, although he also sustains a Platonic view that only the eternal *has* an unalterable identity and is fully *non aliud*. Finite things, though they exclude, and cannot be their opposites, are also involved in an infinite shifting 'approximation', and ceaselessly tend towards the opposite of what they are. For this reason, that which exceeds the law of identity also alone upholds it. In effect Nicholas' specifically post-nominalist view brings more fully to view a modification of Platonism in terms of the infinitude of the absolute which is specifically a consequence of the idea of a 'single' (but not individual) God with unlimited power (pure *possest* or *posse* for Cusa) to effect being as such.

Secondly, Cusa's interest in human participation in divine creative power can also be related to Scotus and Ockham. Given their affirmation of univocity, they tend to say, unlike Aquinas, that creatures can fully bring about being. Hence Ockham says that human beings in a sense create (*QQ*, 2.9). Nicholas says this too, but he restores the creaturely bringing about of being in a finite thing to the context of participation and mediation that still sees being as really an effect of God alone. Nevertheless, in the wake of the nominalists, he talks explicitly of human acts of creation in a way that Aquinas and Bonaventure did not, even if their thought does indicate a human participation in the process of *creatio continua*.

In the third place, Nicholas also realized, following the nominalists, that universals are indeed constructed through language, but that 'fictionalized' universals may still exhibit something that holds in reality, albeit in a more 'conjectural' fashion than acknowledged hitherto. Dietrich of Freibourg and Ulrich of Strasbourg, as Alain de Libera notes, sought to save the Dominican realist legacy by speaking of a purely internal mental construction of the universal, so at once returning to Plotinus and anticipating idealism.[31] But by pursuing a more Proclean, theurgic path (that had always stressed the descent of the ideal in external liturgical and symbolic guises) in a new linguistic mode, Cusa instead opened out a new space for rhetoric, poetics and the human fabricatedness of history. If Boulnois is right in saying that the Thomist paradox of the supernatural is in part inspired by the Aristotelian maxim 'art imitates nature', since for grace, as with art, a sustaining of nature also exceeds and completes it, then the new Cusan space suggests a more explicit coincidence of grace with the art that is intellect.

Such a coincidence, despite de Certeau, *is* found with certain exponents of sacred rhetoric. In, for example, the work of the Lutheran Mathias Flaccius Illyricus, rhetoric is not reduced to ornament and propagandistic manipulation, nor is traditional fourfold exegesis totally abandoned. Instead one finds here a fusion of a human rhetoric that sustains a Longinian interest in the ways words can both reveal and enact through performance the real (Longinus may have been close to theurgic neo-Platonism), with a continued acknowledgment of the divine real rhetoric in allegory.[32] The anagogic here continues to 'produce' the past in the older sense of 'lead forth', but this production includes now also a moment of the creative 'production' of truth in words. Through a blending of Longinus with Augustine's rhetorical writings that was oft repeated by both Protestant and Catholic writers, the indwelling of the Spirit is rethought in terms of a doctrine of poetic inspiration. The biblical writings themselves are considered by Flaccius Illyricus in terms of a human rhetorical construction as well as a divine allegory of the real. This was possible in terms of a Longinian perspective that saw the style with the most sublimely persuasive 'coiled force' to be a 'brief', albeit figurative style, full of *res* and a minimum of *verba*. Such a fusion of human and divine rhetoric carries right through to the Anglicans John Dennis and Robert Lowth in the seventeenth and eighteenth centuries, and thence to the North German Hamann, and many in the nineteenth century, both Catholic and Protestant, influenced by him.[33]

All such people indicate how, in times of diminution, our task is not *only* to recover the pre-1300 vision, but also to acknowledge human consensus, cooperation and varied free poetic power in a way this vision did not fully envisage. High medievalism needs to be supplemented by a Christian socialism, conceived in the widest sense. Theologians who may be the last of the last still have a task before them.

This chapter is dedicated to the Archbishop of Wales, Rowan Williams

Notes

1   See Graham White (1994), *Luther as Nominalist*, Helsinki: Luther-Agricola Society, pp.231–99; Henry Chadwick (1987), 'Philoponus the Christian Theologian', in Richard

Sorabji (ed.), *Philoponus and the Refection of Aristotelian Science*, London: Duckworth; William of Ockham, *Quodlibetal Questions*, 5.10.

2   See Michel de Certeau (1992), *The Mystic Fable*, trans. Michael B. Smith, Chicago: Chicago University Press; Eric Alliez (1996), *Capital Times*, trans. G. van dem Abbeele, Minneapolis: Minnesota University Press.

3   Henri de Lubac (1946), *Surnaturel*, Paris: Aubier; (1967), *The Mystery of the Supernatural*, trans. Rosemary Sheed, London: Chapman. See also Jean-Ives Lacoste (1995), 'Le Désir et L'Inexigible: Préambules à une Lecture', *Les Etudes Philosophiques*, 2, 226–43; and Olivier Boulnois (1995), 'Les deux Fins de L'Homme', *Les Etudes Philosophiques*, 2, 205–22.

4   John Milbank and Catherine Pickstock (2001), *Truth in Aquinas*, London: Routledge.

5   See John Montag SJ (1999), 'Revelation: The False Legacy of Suarez', in J. Milbank, C. Pickstock and G. Ward (eds), *Radical Orthodoxy: A New Theology*, London: Routledge, pp.38–64.

6   See Olivier Boulnois (1999), *Etre et Représentation: Une généalogie de la Métaphysique Moderne à L'Epoque de Duns Scot (xiii–xiv siècle)*, Paris: PUF, pp.463ff.

7   Boulnois, *Etre et Représentation*.

8   Boulnois, 'Les deux Fins de l'Homme'.

9   Michael Buckley (1987), *At the Origins of Modern Atheism*, New Haven: Yale University Press; Jean-Luc Marion (1977), *L'Idole et La Distance*, Paris: Grasset et Fasquelle.

10 Hans Urs von Balthasar (1989), *The Glory of the Lord: A Theological Aesthetics Vol V: The Realm of Metaphysics in the Modern Age*, trans. Brian McNeil *et al.*, London: Sheed and Ward.

11 See Lacoste.

12 John Paul II (1998), *Faith and Reason*, London: Catholic Truth Society.

13 Hans urs von Balthasar (1977), *Love Alone: the Way of Revelation*, London: Sheed and Ward.

14 Thomas Torrance (1980), 'Creation and Science', in *The Ground and Grammar of Theology*, Charlottesville: University of Virginia Press, pp.144–75; (1981), 'The Theology of Light', in *Christian Theology and Scientific Culture*, New York: Oxford University Press. This is a decisive essay for the theology of the future. But one must of course, unlike Torrance, admit fully Grosseteste's neo-Platonism and escape his straining at the limits of Calvinism.

15 Jean-Luc Marion (1991), *God Without Being*, trans. Thomas A. Carlson, Chicago: University of Chicago Press, pp.139–61.

16 Henri de Lubac (1946), *Corpus Mysticum: L'Eucharistie et L'Eglise au Moyen Age*, Paris: Aubier-Montaigne. See also Catherine Pickstock (1998), *After Writing: On the Liturgical Consummation of Philosophy*, Oxford: Blackwell, pp.121–67.

17 De Certeau, *The Mystic Fable*, pp.79–113.

18 Pickstock, *After Writing*, pp.158–66.

19 I am indebted to conversations with Augustine Thompson OP of the University of Virginia on this matter. See also Jean-Yves Lacoste (1998), 'Etre', in Jean-Yves Lacoste (ed.), *Dictionnaire Critique de Théologie*, Paris: PUF.

20 This is how I am inclined to interpret some of Eamon Duffy's evidence. It seems to me that Duffy takes less account than Bossy and Scarisbrick of a late mediaeval decadence itself inaugurating tendencies that early modernity will intensify, because he wishes mainly to argue that Catholicism was in good shape upon the eve of the Reformation. In this respect his position is less complex than that of the two other writers. See Eamon Duffy (1992), *The Stripping of the Altars: Traditional Religion in England 1400–1580*, New Haven: Yale University Press; John Bossy (1985), *Christianity in the West 1400–1700*, Oxford: Oxford University Press; J.J. Scarisbrick (1984), *The Reformation and the English People*, Oxford: Blackwell.

21 I am indebted to discussions with Alison Milbank about this topic.

22 For a summary and synthesis of their views, see Pickstock, *After Writing*.

23 Nicholas of Cusa (1995), *The Catholic Concordance*, trans. Paul E. Sigmund, Cambridge: Cambridge University Press.
24 Augustine, *Ad Hesychium* (PL 33, p.913), cited by Nicholas in Book I, para. 14.
25 Cusa, *The Catholic Concordance*, Book I, paras 56–9.
26 Cusa, *The Catholic Concordance*, Book III, paras 294–312.
27 Cusa, *The Catholic Concordance*, Book I, para. 14.
28 I am indebted here to the unpublished work of Peter Candler of Duke University.
29 See de Certeau, *The Mystic Fable*, p.222, citing the work of Pier Cesari Bori on Gregory the Great's reading of Ezekiel's vision.
30 William of Ockham, *Quodlibetal Questions*, 5.12 and 14. Cusa's interest in human participation in divine creative power can also be related to Scotus and Ockham.
31 Alain de Libera (1984), *Introduction à la Mystique Rhénane*, Paris: PUF.
32 See Debora Shuger (1988), *Sacred Rhetoric: The Christian Grand Style in the English Renaissance*, Princeton, NJ: Princeton University Press, pp.73–6.
33 See John Milbank (1997), 'Pleonasm, Speech and Writing', in *The Word Made Strange*, Oxford: Blackwell, pp.55–84.

Chapter 7

A Lived Theology

Jürgen Moltmann

My Way to Theology

Things in my life have generally turned out differently from what I intended. I wanted to study physics and mathematics, following the heroes of my youth in Planck, Bohr, Einstein and de Broglie. Then, when I was 17, only by a miracle I survived the firestorm that destroyed my hometown of Hamburg in July 1943 during the RAF's bombing operation 'Gomorrah'. Fifty thousand people died on the last night of the bombing, including my friend Gerhard Schopper who was blown to pieces at my side. That night I cried out to God for the first time: 'Where is God?', 'Why am I not dead too?' and 'What am I alive for?' These questions are still with me today. To find an answer to them became more important for me than the formula $e = mc^2$.

When the battle for Arnhem in Holland began in the autumn of 1944, we recruits, barely trained as we were, were thrown into the front at Helmond. After the first armoured attack in Asten, only half my company were still alive. In 1945, I was taken prisoner at Cleves by English soldiers, and liberated – at least from lice! The war's end in May 1945 meant that we POWs looked forward to going home. But for me that homecoming was delayed by three long years, until 1948. First came a labour camp in Kilmarnock (Scotland), followed by Norton Camp, run by the YMCA, and founded by the Swedish pastor Birger Forell. There I began to study theology, to the disappointment of my humanist father, who thought that his meek son was about to turn Catholic and even become a monk. However, what I wanted was to get an answer to my questioning about God, and to find out what was true about faith in Christ. For me, everything in theology was fabulously new and in fact this is still so today. My religiosity is nothing more than theological curiosity.

In April 1948, I returned to Hamburg, to the damaged home of my parents, a city full of refugees. Soon after, I left for Göttingen's university as our local pastor, Helmut Traub, a first generation Barthian, put me in touch with Ernst Wolf. Initially in Göttingen I slept in the seminar cloakroom, ate a subsidized student lunch for a few pence (though it had to be before 11 o'clock), and in the evenings listened by candlelight to Professor Iwand lectures on Luther's theology. It was a wonderful time. We lived only 'the life of the mind', greedy to catch up with everything we had missed. My father financed eight semesters, giving me 100DM a month. That money set my time limit for my studies.

After two semesters I fell in love with Elisabeth Wendel, a doctoral student of Otto Weber's, and in order to be near her I asked him to give me a subject for a doctorate. He gave me 'Moyse Amyraut and the theological school of Saumur', a topic that was completely unknown to me, and which kept me busy. In 1952, I sat my theological exams, had my doctoral *viva*, and got married all within a fortnight. I took on rather too much, but things still have not changed in that regard.

In Göttingen then, the previous theological 'struggle' between the Confessing Church and the German Christians still raged or, to be more exact, the dispute between Iwand and Gogarten raged. When the American troops marched in, Emmanuel Hirsch, the mastermind of the German Christians (and the Nazis), withdrew to his own company. We, nonetheless, under Iwand, struggled with Gogarten's secularization theory, and tried to translate the experiences and theology of the politically resistant Confessing Church into the post-war era. But the political restorations of Adenauer and Otto Dibelius' understanding of the Protestant church eventually defeated our teachers and us. Our concern switched to reconciling Barth and Bultmann, the elephant and the whale, as they termed each other. Götz Harbsmeier, Hermann Diem, Ernst Wolf and Walter Kreck did their best to assist us. We students struggled with 'demythologization' and 'immanent Trinity', attempting to reconcile them. There was a real theological culture of dispute, before controversy degenerated into disorderly dialogue, and dialogue turned into trivial pluralism, eventually falling silent altogether. Ernst Käsemann, coming to Göttingen in 1951, also brought additional controversy with his apocalyptic passion of the truth of the justification of the godless 'and only the godless'. My own biblical teachers, Joachim Jeremias and Gerhard von Rad, were far milder and had a more lasting influence on me.

Theology in the Pastorate

In our youthful kingdom-of-God idealism, newly married as we were, we wanted to go to the eastern zone of Germany, the GDR (my wife came from Potsdam), to try to build up a congregation in one of the heavily destroyed regions. We waited in West Berlin all summer as four entry visa applications were rejected because I had been a prisoner in British hands (not Russian ones) and so I might have been a spy. I tried to work as a hospital chaplain, completely new ground for me, while my wife taught the nurses. We felt at home in a group called the *Unterwegskreis* (People on the Move), which was critical of the political scene and equally critical of the church. We were sent back to West Germany in the autumn of 1952, and Otto Weber found me a job as curate in the remotest corner of Germany one can think of, in Wittgenstein, beyond Erndtebrück. There I visited remote forest villages on skis, armed with the Bible and a few herrings, often carrying needed provisions in my rucksack. I spent the summer of 1953 with my friend Johannes Kuhn in the Reformed seminary at Elberfeld, perfecting my table tennis and learning to sing metrical psalms. After that, again through Otto Weber's intervention, I accepted a call to a pastorate in Bremen-Wasserhorst, which lay on a dyke on the River Wumme (a tributary of the Weser) near Bremen: 7 miles long, 60 farms, 500 people, 3000 cows, 20 per cent churchgoers, 80 per cent communicants, with all the village youth in the youth group and a women's meeting for old and young.

The gap between two theologians equipped with doctorates and this village congregation was immense. Luckily, living in barracks and army huts had made me a practised card player, bridging the gap between 'scholar' and 'farmer'. In the little church of Wasserhorst I learned to preach to many or to fewer people. I found this difficult, for I had never heard any sermons when I was young, and was not a particularly gifted speaker. Those were hard years but good ones, in a manse with eight rooms, though initially we only used a corner of one of them. We heated the place with primitive iron stoves, were flooded, had rats in the cellar, mice in the kitchen, owls under the roof and wild cattle in the unkempt garden. During our five years there, our first children were born and I had time during the mornings, following Otto Weber's advice, to write a book on Christoph Pezel and Bremen's transition to Calvinism in the sixteenth century.

In 1957, at Göttingen, at Weber's suggestion once more, I started working on my habilitation (professorial thesis). That year, every Wednesday morning, having breakfasted on the train, I held my first poorly attended lectures on the history of Reformed (Calvinist) theology. My farmers reacted to my departure realistically, thinking it an improvement of my situation. I, on the other hand, was not certain that this move to 'academia' was for the best at the time. I would have preferred to move to a bigger congregation in Bremerhaven. I was not cut out to be a professional pastor, but I liked being confronted with the whole breadth and depth of life – children and old people, men and women, the healthy and the sick, birth and death. I should, in hindsight, have liked as a theologian to remain a pastor.

At Göttingen I had turned from being a 'despairing but consoled' follower of Kierkegaard into a Barthian sworn to the *Barmen Declaration*. I saw no future for systematic theology after Barth, any more than there could still be philosophy after Hegel. Barth had said it all, and said it so well. I was freed from this heresy in 1956–7, at a theological conference, where I met the Dutch theologian Arnold van Ruler and got to know his theology of the apostolate, and his kingdom of God theology: 'I smell a rose, and smell the kingdom of God.' I sensed then that there was something else after all which the Grand Old Man of Basle had not already done.

Theology at the *Kirchliche Hochschule*, Wuppertal

In 1958, I began to teach in Wuppertal with Rudolf Bohren. We were brought there by the invitation of the Old Testament scholar Hans Walter Wolff. We were a young faculty, including Wolfhart Pannenberg and the New Testament scholar Georg Eichholz, and had begun to develop our own theology, without looking over our shoulders at tradition and the great who had preceded us. Two eventual examples of this youthful iconoclasm were Pannenberg's *Revelation as History* and my *Theology of Hope*. We were politically involved, putting our proverbial oars into the new waters of the time, away from the era of German restoration and the existentialism of the 1950s. In 1958, the whole faculty drew up a protest against the atom bomb. I also signed the *Ten Brotherhood Theses* on behalf of peace drawn up by Barth. In 1961, together with Hans-Ulrich Kirchhoff, I compiled and published a book on *The Beginnings of Dialectical Theology*, which won me the reputation of being dialectical theology's 'keeper of the Grail'. It was also while in Wuppertal that I met Ernst Bloch, then in Leipzig, for the first time, and also Carl Schmitt, Arnold Gehlen, Rut Fischer, Walter Jens and Gottfried Benn. All were part of a continuing project by Dr Leeb to bring scholars to Wuppertal to engage in dialogue on current cultural affairs.

Then, while I was on holiday in Switzerland, I read Ernst Bloch's *Principle of Hope*, and was fascinated. I wondered why theology had let hope, its very own theme, slip through its fingers. Ideas for a theology of hope began to ferment. I tried them out in lectures in Wuppertal and Bonn in 1963, and published them in 1964 as my *Theology of Hope*. There is no need to go into that any further. I was bowled over by the worldwide response. I only recovered from it in 1967, after I had moved to Tübingen. I chased after my own shadow, with lectures throughout the country and all over the world, and had no more time for my family. After this came my interest in the Christian–Marxist dialogue (which took place for the last time in May 1968 in Marienbad) and with it my friendship with Johann Baptist Metz. Bloch had brought us together when we met on the occasion of his eightieth birthday. I also struck up friendships during that time with the Czechoslovakian theologians Milan Machovec and Viteslav Gardavsky. My life was breathtakingly exciting and time consuming. In 1961, Ernst Wolf invited me to join the board of the periodical *Evangelische Theologie*, and at its meetings the great theological controversies between the old theological schools and the new generations of young theologians were fought out.

Theology in State Universities

In 1963, I was invited to a chair in Bonn and, as German universities come under the regional ministries of education, effectively became a civil (or state) servant. I did so with considerable hesitation, for what had happened during the dictatorship of the Third Reich was still too vivid a memory. I found Bonn personally difficult. For example, Gerhard Gloege was friendly, whereas Walter Kreck, perhaps feeling under attack and harbouring a Barthian mistrust of the newcomer, was not so friendly. I was friendly with the Catholic moral theologian Franz Böckle and the two of us attended and addressed a number of medical congresses. I was a young member of an old faculty, but I acquired my first doctoral students, all of them of mature years now.

In 1966, my situation became complicated. Otto Weber died, and I was to take over his chair in Göttingen, but had no wish to do so. Ernst Käsemann, however, entreated me, with the apocalyptic fervour of a Farel to the young Calvin, to come to Tübingen. I gave in, to the longstanding regret of my wife, and went to Tübingen. We arrived in Tübingen for the summer semester of 1967, but initially only for that one brief semester, since a year at Duke University, North Carolina, had already been planned.

We travelled via Paris, so as to say *au revoir* to European culture, and then crossed on the *France* to New York, where we lost ourselves in the labyrinth of Manhattan. Afterwards we flew to North Carolina, a place of pine trees and golf courses – and black ghettoes. I found lecturing in English difficult, and only managed with the help of my American assistant and faithful friend, Doug Meeks. Our four children gamely struggled with American schools, finding them no easier than American children did our schools in Tübingen. In 1967, the English translation of my *Theology of Hope* appeared, and was reviewed on the front page of the *New York Times*, under the heading: '"God is Dead" Doctrine Losing Ground to Theology of Hope'. 'You've made it,' said my wide-eyed American students to me.

At the beginning of April 1968, as a farewell, a great symposium was held at Duke on the *Theology of Hope*. At its climax, Harvey Cox burst into the lecture room crying, 'Martin Luther King has been shot!' The American ghettoes went up in flames and in many American cities a state of emergency was declared. All the conference participants flew home as quickly as possible. Then something unforgettable happened. Our Duke students, otherwise so slow and hard to move, set up a demonstration. Four hundred students, men and women, sat in the quad for six days and six nights, part of the time in rain, and mourned Martin Luther King. On the sixth day, black students from a nearby college arrived, danced through the rows, and sat down beside the white students. After a while we all began to sing, in tears: 'We shall overcome . . . someday.'

Deeply moved by our American experience, we returned to Tübingen in late April of 1968. In Berlin at that time the student leader Rudi Dutschke had been shot, just as Martin Luther King had been in America. In Tübingen as well student protests raged. It was said to be due to them, and not because of me, that Gerhard Ebeling withdrew to Zürich and Joseph Ratzinger to Regensburg, where 'all was (still) right with the world'. I went with the students, trying to understand them, and because of this I experienced discord and disagreement with most members of the faculty. But, although I knew Marx well, I was not a Marxist, so I was also *persona non grata* with the students. I was under fire from both sides, and could not please anyone. Even the 'radical' political theology that I developed and supported, together with Johann Baptist Metz, was not radical enough for the radical students – or, for that matter, later for the Latin American liberation theologians. At that time I wanted to write my 'Ethics of Hope', but nothing came of it because I first wished to deepen my theology of hope dialectically with the theology of the cross. In 1971, in order to be free from the moral pressure of political events and ideas, my assistant, Marcel Martin, wrote his book on play, while I published the little book called in English *Theology and Joy*.

During the 1970s, through the World Council of Churches' 'Faith and Order Commission' (to which I had belonged since 1963) and through book translations, I acquired international contacts with black theology in the United States, liberation theology in Latin America, *Minjung* theology in Korea, African theology and *Kairos* theology in South Africa and, astonishingly enough, Orthodox theology in Romania. In 1979, following Walter Kasper's dissociation from Hans Küng, I became one of the directors of *Concilium* and, together with Küng, was one of the editors of this ecumenical periodical until 1994. I travelled more than was good for my lectures and seminary in Tübingen or, for that matter, for my family. Following Ernst Wolf's death, I took over the editorship of the periodical *Evangelische Theologie*, and became president of the *Gesellschaft für Evangelische Theologie*.

Looking back, it is a curious thing about theology that problems come up, are discussed to the point of personal recrimination (at least in Germany) and then, still unresolved, quietly disappear again, pensioned off, so to speak. Over my career, what was controversial in the 1950s was 'the secularized society', while the 1960s raged against the capitalist society from a Frankfurt school neo-Marxist critique. Later, in the mid-1970s, 'revolution' gave way to 'religion', and with it came interfaith dialogue. Eberhard Jüngel and I had just battled with revolutionary atheism when our friend Hans Küng came along, already arm-in-arm with the world religions, and laid down the new agenda. The 1980s saw the 'Me decade', with its inner search for identity and its new thrust towards individualization in Western society. In the 'First World' the apparent 'revolution of the soul' has replaced the previous generation's penchant for 'revolution in society'. This is most clearly seen by the fact that books on personal problems and counselling now oust theological books in the seminary. The esoteric has taken over from the theological. Finally, and not least of all, the new feminist theology emerged, and 'pushed' us men aside.

I think it was in 1977 at a conference in Mexico City that I suddenly realized, 'You're not black, so black theology is not for you; you're not oppressed, so you can't be a liberation theologian; and you're not a woman, so for you feminist theology is not a possibility.' As this became clear, although I supported these new contextual theologies to the best of my ability, I myself withdrew into a productive disengagement and concentrated on long-term theological problems. So I began my 'systematic contributions' to theology, surprising both friends and foes with a first volume on the social doctrine of the Trinity. I continued with a doctrine of creation, *God in Creation*. This fitted with the ecological trend of the time, although my intention was not to write a trendy theology. After that I really wanted to stop, thinking I had now said everything I had to say. Lectures and seminars also became somewhat burdensome. I found, however, that the closer I came to the end of my academic life, the more I came to enjoy the companionship of my students, graduate students and my assistants.

So I began anew with fresh courage and enthusiasm. Things developed rapidly and unrelentingly. In 1989, I published my Christology under the title *The Way of Jesus Christ: Christology in Messianic Dimensions*. It was intended to be a Christology for the wandering people of God, and closely related to Israel. *The Spirit of Life: A Universal Affirmation* followed in 1991. It was neither planned nor announced. I wrote it for pure pleasure, inspired or 'inspirited', and with great enthusiasm.

German professors have to retire at the age of 68. I drained the last drop of the joys and burdens of academic life until my last day in 1994. After a terrific farewell party in Tübingen, I discovered that the pleasures of academic life remained; and that it was only the burdens that I was able to shake off on retiring. Life went on as before: reading and writing, travelling and talking.

In 1995, my major book *The Coming of God: Christian Eschatology* was finished and published. With it, what I had begun in 1964 with the *Theology of Hope* came full circle. In the earlier book, my intention had been to show the vital power of hope in action; now I wanted to present the future we can hope for if we believe: eternal life – the kingdom of God – the new creation of all things – the glory of God. After these five major books, I felt bound to close with a book about method. Usually, reflections about method are to be found in the *prolegomena* to one's dogmatics, but since I had begun with an eschatology, it seemed appropriate enough to put my ideas about the methods and systems of theology in an *epilegomena*. It is said that reflections on method are like clearing one's throat before a lecture and anyone who spends too long over it will lose his audience. I myself have always been more fascinated by theological ideas and subjects than by reflections about the intellectual ways of getting alongside them. In 1999, the sixth and last volume in the series of my 'systematic contributions' to theology appeared, under the title *Experiences in Theology: Ways and Forms of Christian Theology*. The book can also be interpreted as an introduction to my theological thinking.

Abraham Lincoln is reported to have said that he had no wish to be the slave of any master or the master of any slave. In a different context, the same could be said of me. I had no wish to be the teacher of students eternally bound to me, or to be the mere student of teachers to whom I was eternally bound. My theology is not designed for repetition. It is intended to stimulate people towards their own theological thinking and their own theological experience. If two people say the same thing, one of them is superfluous. When the teacher–pupil relationship ends, what follows, if it was a good relationship, is a friendship of mutual affection and respect. In theology we are all pupils of One who is greater than ourselves. 'How small is that with which we struggle, how great is that which strives with us,' says Rilke in his

Book of Hours. Our finest theological systems are finally no more than fragments, and our best methods are ultimately misconceived. The truth of God is best shown in the broken threads and new beginnings of our theology. I have also experienced the truth of T.S. Eliot's line 'in my end is my beginning' again and again both in my life and in my theological thinking, making me humble – and curious. I conclude with some final thoughts about theology and the pastor or theologian given to my Tübingen students on my retirement in 1994.

Theology as a Passion

Theology has nothing to do with 'religious management' studies. Theology is a passion that one pursues with all one's heart, all one's soul and all one's strength. If one cannot do that, better to leave it alone altogether. Theology comes from the passion of God, from the open wound of God in one's own life, from Job's indictment of God and the accusing cry of the crucified Christ to God, from the absence of God, and experiences of 'the sufferings of this present time', whether Auschwitz, Stalingrad, Vietnam, Bosnia or Chernobyl, without end.

Theology springs from unbounded joy in the presence of God's Spirit, the Spirit of the resurrection, so that one affirms this life with the whole, undivided love of God and despite life's devastations one still loves, being 'there' as present, wholly present. That capacity is God's own delight in life.

God's pain and God's delight, consequently, are the two experiences between which theology is kept in suspense. I wish you, as students of theology, suffering from God and a delight in God – namely passion for the kingdom of God.

Theology as a Personal Conviction

Secondly, we are theologians wholly and completely or not at all. Theology is not a religious profession we practise only while we are 'on duty' and then do something quite different in our private life. We have to do with the 'ultimate things', the very things by which people stand or fall. Do not ask: 'What will the bishop or the superintendent say?', 'What will the congregation say?' or 'What will my colleagues or the media say?' Likewise, do not ask: 'Can I be sure of general assent?', 'Am I qualifying myself for a call or appointment?' or even 'Am I generally well liked?' Faith is personal conviction. It is only personal conviction that can support us in life and in death, raise us up, console and accompany us in life and vocation: 'I know that my Redeemer lives.'

We do not have to believe every dogma and every article in the creed. Every Christian has a fundamental right to doubt – every Christian and every pastor or theologian too. But, of course, we can and must give ourselves time as well. No one understands everything all at once. There are degrees of importance and steps in understanding. Nonetheless, the right to liberty of conscience requires us not to speak or act against conscience and conviction under any circumstance, no matter how daunting or costly the task ahead.

Theology as Imagination for the Kingdom of God

You are going to be pastors or theologians affiliated with various institutional churches. In Germany, our *Volkskirche*, our established model of assuming 'responsibility' for all souls in the parish, is an outdated model. People are leaving the mainline church in droves, no longer wanting a pastor to 'look over' them, or wanting to be affiliated with the church simply because they 'live' nearby it. The end looks, for Germany (and elsewhere), to be a 'people's church' model without people. For example, church membership in East Berlin is less than 10 per cent. In the former East Germany membership is 20 per cent on average. A dramatic new drive towards individualization and a corresponding decline in religious affiliation means you will no longer be 'running a parish', 'looking after a congregation' or 'celebrating religious rituals from the cradle to the grave'. Instead, you will be *gathering* a congregation and *building* it up. You will be living with the 'un-churched' and talking about faith with the godless. Do not withdraw into your own little group or ghetto. Go, instead, to the people who are far off and to the godless. It is there that you, as pastor or theologian, will become assured of your own faith. While we do not know what form the church of Christ will take once the *Volkskirche* and the like model is finally at an end, I am certain that every end conceals a new beginning, because God always hides his new beginnings in the end of what is old, and in the crises of the old we find the chances for the new. In the church reforms of the last 40 years my generation developed ideas about a congregational church, a participatory church, a voluntary church, and accordingly emphasized these transitory things. You do not have to take any notice of them alone. You will discover the new beginnings of Christ's church for yourselves, if you only look for them. Seek first the kingdom of God and his righteousness and justice in the world; then the living congregation and the open church will be added unto you, just of themselves.

Finally, I wish you imagination for the kingdom of God. The Gospel offers inspiration enough. We only need the courage to find it for ourselves.

(Translated by Margaret Kohl)

Chapter 8

A Theological Pilgrimage

Gerald O'Collins SJ

The invitation to write for this book forced a number of questions on me: which people and what circumstances have influenced me theologically over the years? What do I expect from Christian theologians? What do I, rightly or wrongly, think that I have contributed?

The Road to Rome

Before I settled down in 1974 as a full-time member of the theology faculty of the Gregorian University in Rome, people in four cities had helped to make possible a vocation to theology and to shape the way I have thought theologically. When I was growing up in Melbourne (Australia), my mother insisted that I begin studying Latin and Greek at the age of 12. Did she think that dead languages were stepping-stones to modern languages, or that they taught the eloquence and sharp logic needed for success in the legal profession that my father had anticipated for me? Mother spoke of Latin and Greek being part of a 'gentleman's education' but offered no further explanation. Without intending to do so, she steered me in a theological direction. The teachers at high school and at the University of Melbourne immersed me in Latin and Greek – to the point of my being able to translate English prose and poetry into those ancient languages without any help from dictionaries. Unfortunately, Hebrew came later; starting to learn it at the age of 29, I have never mastered it properly.

At the University of Melbourne, strong departments of philosophy and history also had their influence on me. Analytic philosophers, many of them trained at the University of Oxford, dominated the campus. They trained me to 'watch my language' and scrutinize statements for any careless imprecision. Such philosophers, sad to say, find such imprecision all too often in current theological writing. For example, recently reading a work on Christology from a leading theologian, I came across the claim: 'no statements about God are informative'. Did he mean that the *only* statement about God that is informative is that all other statements about God are non-informative? Or had he forgotten to add a crucial adverb: 'no statements about God are *merely* informative'? The former proposition looks self-contradictory; the latter is perfectly acceptable. The analytic philosophers in Melbourne and their teachers in Oxford rightly found some theological writing carelessly inexact. But their philosophy, so I found, could be nicely wedded to the transcendental Thomism I was also learning from Joseph Maréchal (1878–1944) and Karl Rahner (1904–84). That school of Thomism argued for the dynamic drive of the human spirit beyond sense perception to the absolute fullness of being in God. The analytic philosophers, while in those days not normally enthusiastic about any forms of Thomism, happily encouraged studies of Plato and Aristotle. I finished my studies at the University of Melbourne with a several hundred-page thesis on some aspects of Aristotle's theory of matter and form. That thesis led to my being granted a travelling scholarship to study at Cambridge. My first book, a biography of my maternal grandfather, Patrick McMahon Glynn (1855–1931), also eased the way to receiving the scholarship. Grandfather had spent years as a member and a minister in state and national parliament, as well as helping to write the Australian constitution.

Although most of my time at the University of Melbourne was spent in the departments of classics and philosophy, I also enjoyed the company and conversation of members of the history department. In a friendly way they passed on something of what the art of historical writing entails. That made it possible to write and publish with Melbourne University Press and Cambridge University Press my first book, *Patrick McMahon Glynn: A Founder of Australian Federation* (1965).

Studies in Germany in the 1960s and 1970s enriched my life and theological thinking through contacts in Tübingen: with Jürgen Moltmann (who became a lasting and dear friend), the late Ernst Bloch, and others including the late Ernst Käsemann, whose lectures on St Paul's *Letter to the Romans* showed how outstanding biblical scholarship incorporated and required deep Christian faith and theological reflection. In Australia I had already been initiated into such a happy blend of faith, theology and exegesis by William Dalton SJ and the late John Scullion SJ. At the University of Cambridge I was to learn the same lesson from Charles Moule: biblical scholarship that lacks faith will be as shallow as literary criticism that is not fuelled by a passionate love for literature. The scriptures were born of faith, aim to gave rise to faith, and should be interpreted with faith.

During my years in Cambridge and especially when I returned for a sabbatical (1973–4), Judith O'Neill, a friend who has published novels and works of literary criticism, generously criticized and corrected what I was writing at the time. More than anyone else, Judy encouraged me to use verbs, shun abstract nouns, and avoid that horribly ponderous language that some theologians indulge. No wonder so much theology fails to have a wider impact! It is badly written and shows little respect for its subject, the tri-personal God revealed in Jesus Christ.

Between finishing my Cambridge PhD in 1968 and starting full-time for the Gregorian University in 1974, I was a visiting professor for Weston School of Theology (Cambridge, Massachusetts). The experience of the greater Boston area, with its rich array of universities that draw students from around the world, along with frequent visits to my sister Maev, who was completing her PhD at Colombia University (New York), fostered a 'catholic' horizon for theology:

one must reflect and act in ways that are truly interracial, intercultural and international. That ideal was reinforced at the Gregorian, where only 30 per cent of the students are Italians, and the rest come from well over 100 countries spread around the world. My Boston and New York experience proved to be a valuable preparation for teaching in Rome.

Resurrection, Revelation and Experience

Teaching courses and running seminars at the Gregorian solidified and clarified previous interests in the larger themes of Christ's resurrection, God's self-revelation and human experience.

My lifelong concern with the resurrection began in 1967, when I was at Pembroke College, Cambridge, and doing my research for a doctorate. I received an urgent telephone call from Henry Hart, the dean of Queens' College, Cambridge, who was looking for someone to deliver a lecture to a small theological society at two days' notice. He did not mind what I spoke about, and on the spur of the moment the only subject I could come up with was the resurrection of Jesus. That eleventh-hour invitation from Henry Hart has kept me thinking about, teaching and writing on the resurrection for over 30 years, and resulted in five books, numerous articles and several dictionary entries. While I obviously retraced ground already trodden by others, I believe that I have been able to contribute additional insights: for instance, concerning the role of St Peter as Easter witness, the nature of the first disciples' encounters with the risen Jesus, and the justification of faith in Jesus as gloriously risen from the dead.

In regard to the interpretation of Peter primarily (but not exclusively) as an Easter witness, some commentators dismiss my thesis as 'Catholic apologetics', ignoring the fact that throughout the twentieth century it has been largely German Protestant scholars who have been willing to examine the special importance of Peter in announcing the resurrection. Some others reject the thesis because they take it to be a denigration of St Mary Magdalene. But I have persistently championed the Gospel traditions that report that women were present at the empty tomb, a tradition which stands or falls with the presence of Mary Magdalene. Can we not honour both Mary Magdalene and Peter among the original Easter witnesses?

In regard to the work I have done on the nature of the first disciples' encounters with the risen Jesus and the validation of our resurrection faith, I received valuable feedback from Peter Carnley, the Anglican Archbishop of Perth (Western Australia) and the American theologian Francis Schüssler Fiorenza at a New York meeting: the Easter Summit of 1996. Archbishop Carnley, in particular, prompted me to give more thought to the possibilities and limits of analogies between the appearances of the risen Jesus and, for example, the documented experiences of contact between widows and widowers and their dead spouses. The discussion with Carnley motivated a contribution to a meeting on the resurrection held at the Roehampton Institute, London, which resulted in the book edited by Stanley Porter and others, *Resurrection* (1999).

When I was working on my doctorate at Cambridge University, 'The Theology of Revelation in Some Recent Discussion', I already found myself obliged to think through such issues as the relationship between (a) God's self-revelation that reached its high point with the coming of Jesus, and (b) the living presence of that revelation as history unfolds and people are called, in one generation after another, to accept in faith the divine self-manifestation which was completed with Jesus and the first disciples. I called (a) 'foundational' revelation and (b) 'dependent' revelation, insisting always that, while (b) added no new content or hitherto unknown truth, it involved the constant renewing of God's revealing word to people now. In my *Has Dogma a Future?* (1975) I queried the usefulness of lumping together as 'dogmas' the essential content of foundational revelation, which church teaching had elucidated over the centuries. In my *Fundamental Theology* (1981) I proposed using 'experience' as the *leitmotif* for interpreting dependent revelation and its transmission through the great tradition and the inspired scriptures.

Among leading protagonists in the discipline of fundamental or foundational theology my proposals received little attention. The distinction between foundational and dependent revelation shaped the thinking of some Gregorian graduate students, and may have rubbed off on readers of *Fundamental Theology* (which in English, Italian, Korean and Portuguese sold well over 20 000 copies). But that was about all. As far as I am aware, no prominent teacher of fundamental theology outside the Gregorian University ever discussed either the distinction between foundational and dependent revelation or the feasibility of experience as the *leitmotif* for that branch of theology. In the bulletin of fundamental theology that he publishes every now and then in the *Revue Thomiste*, Jean-Pierre Torrell once or twice has drawn his readers' attention to my proposal about experience. But that was it for many years, until Daniel Kendall and Stephen Davis hosted 21 scholars in a *Festschrift* of my work and career. The resultant publication, *The Convergence of Theology*, was published in 2001.

My interest in religious experience fuelled my desire to write in the area of spirituality and to do so for general, non-specialist readers. From the 1970s into the 1980s, James Walsh, the founding editor of the British journal of spirituality, *The Way*, regularly asked me to contribute. A concern about spiritual experience also lay behind many of the articles I have written for the London *Tablet* and *America* magazine, as well as prompting me to publish *The Second Journey* (1978), *A Month with Jesus* (1978), *Finding Jesus* (1983), *Experiencing Jesus* (1994), *All Things New* (1998) and *Following the Way* (1999).

After Moltmann had inspired me to write on the experience of hope in the late 1960s, the experience of love and hatred entered my thinking in the area of redemption: the salvation offered by Christ and his Spirit to a world constantly wounded by the forces of hatred. It has continued to surprise me that most modern theologians have paid little attention to love as *the* clue to the whole drama of creation and redemption and no attention at all to hatred, the opposite of love. Yet Christianity offers a uniquely rich tradition of reflection upon love, and classical thinkers like St Thomas Aquinas also wrestled with the theme of hatred, a malignant sore which remains so widely present in human society.

Presence and Summits

Three American scholars, in particular, fed my thinking and work during the last years of the second millennium and the opening years of the third: William Kelly, Stephen Davis and Daniel Kendall.

For his Gregorian doctoral dissertation, Father Bill Kelly worked with me on the possibilities of 'presence' as a *leitmotif* for Christological reflection. We shared our findings and reflections. Bill happily defended his thesis, and I produced my first book for Oxford University Press, *Christology: A Biblical, Historical and Systematic Study of Jesus* (1995). I used the theme of 'presence' to pull together my views on the person and the redemptive mission of Jesus. Feedback from some reviewers has prompted me to develop further that theme, which has hardly ever been deployed in systematic Christological thinking.

My first Gregorian doctoral student, Dan Kendall, defended his thesis in 1975 and later collaborated with me in writing various articles and books. I had always wanted to stage an interdisciplinary, international and ecumenical meeting of scholars on the resurrection of Jesus. With Dan and Steve Davis, a philosopher friend from Claremont McKenna College (California), I organized such a meeting in New York during Easter of 1996. Oxford University Press published the proceedings the following year as *The Resurrection: An Interdisciplinary Symposium on the Resurrection of Jesus*. Many of the reviews proved encouragingly positive, and so other 'Summits' followed, with 20 or so biblical scholars, theologians, philosophers, patristic scholars and experts in other disciplines (like Christian ethics, homiletics and religious art) joining us. The contributions to the Easter 1998 'Trinity Summit' were published the following year as *The Trinity*. The 2000 proceedings of the Easter 'Incarnation Summit' will appear in 2002 as *The Incarnation*.

As I write, preparations are underway for a final 'Summit' meeting during Easter of 2003: the Redemption Summit. With that meeting, I hope to conclude our interdisciplinary symposia on core Christian beliefs: the resurrection, the Trinity, the incarnation and the redemption.

Looking back on my pilgrimage, I end with three pieces of advice. First, the same persevering prayer that allows one's life to be sustained by God's grace must nourish theology. Without such, theologians cannot expect to exhibit deep integrity in their thinking and living. Second, theology moves ahead only through the collaborative interaction that makes it possible and even easy to explore, grasp and practise truth together. Third, constant dialogue with the best biblical scholarship and philosophical thought available remains as essential as ever. Those who have shared in the three 'Easter Summits' exemplify strikingly the advice I have just given.

Chapter 9

An Intellectual Autobiography

Rosemary Radford Ruether

I sometimes describe my process of intellectual work as spiralling, rather than changing or going from one topic to another. In my corpus of some 35 books and hundreds of articles written from the mid-1960s to today it seems as if I have addressed a vast array of issues: the Church (especially Roman Catholicism), feminism, anti-Semitism, racism against African–Americans, Latin American liberation theology, Christian theological history from women's perspective, the mistreatment of Palestinians by the state of Israel, ecology, family and Buddhist–Christian dialogue. For me, these many issues are deeply interconnected. Most of them have been present in my thinking since the late 1960s or early 1970s. Early book collections of essays, such as *Liberation Theology: Human Hope Confronts Christian History and American Power* (1972) address most of them. Particular books which focus on one or another of these issues are more of a deepening process than a change of focus.

I grew up in a family that was simultaneously Roman Catholic and ecumenical, and I have expanded but maintained that combination. My mother was a Roman Catholic of English and Austro-Hungarian extraction who was born in Mexico in 1895 and grew up there and in Southern California. She took her religion seriously, with regular prayer, daily mass and serious reading, but had little patience with what she saw as 'vulgar Catholicism', superstition or clerical authoritarianism. She passed on to me a sense that the tradition should be taken seriously, but still thought about freely and critically. For example, nuns and priests who try to make you feel guilty about asking questions should be disregarded as backward and uneducated. The ghetto mentality of many Catholics growing up in the 1940s to 1950s in the United States was largely absent from my experience.

My father was an Episcopalian whose religion was more a social and class identity than a personal experience. I remember him dressing up to go to Trinity Episcopal church in Washington DC where his family had belonged for generations, and sometimes went with him on the few times he went to church, Christmas and Easter. I grew up assuming that his church was to be respected. However, in terms of seriousness or personal commitment, there was not much contest between my mother's and my father's religion. My favourite uncle, David Sandow, was a Jew whose religion was more a culture than a personal practice. A skilled musician and painter, he acted as a kind of surrogate father to my sisters and myself when my father was away during the Second World War. He imbued us with a lifelong love of the arts.

To this diversity of immediate family religious cultures others added a sense of outreach and other possibilities. My great aunt was married to a Russian diplomat and lived for many decades in St Petersburg. She was a writer and playwright who published on Russian folk stories and on her own family history and was partial to both Russian Orthodoxy and spiritualism. When both her husband and son died suddenly, she cultivated spiritualist contact with them and published a book on her experiences called *There are no Dead* (1912). After my father's death in 1948, we moved to Southern California. There several of my mother's socially engaged women friends attended Quaker meeting, appreciating their pacifist stance. I went with them from time to time, while also attending mass with my mother. Thereby I imbibed the assumption that one can immerse oneself in several religious traditions at once without having to choose between them, as if they were mutually exclusive.

During my teen years I cultivated the fine arts, with the mentoring of my uncle David and aspired to be an artist. From 1964 to 1968, I attended Scripps College in Claremont, California, a school that focused on the fine arts and the humanities. I began as an art major but was drawn into the classics by a charismatic teacher, Robert Palmer. I began to take Latin and Greek, as well as French and German, and to immerse myself in the literature, history and philosophy of ancient Greece and Rome. My mentors in classics were partial to the history of religions approach to the study of Greco-Roman culture. With them I read authors such as Jane Harrison and Gilbert Murray and investigated the ancient religious origins of Greek tragedy. From these classical studies the religious question emerged as predominant: 'How did Christianity, an unlikely apocalyptic Jewish sect, manage to win, to gather up all of ancient culture in a new synthesis by the fourth century CE?'

My teachers, such as Robert Palmer, did not particularly appreciate Christianity. He thought it was rather a shame that it 'won'. I remember him saying sadly, when speaking of the neo-Platonic systems that rivalled Christianity briefly under the emperor Julian, 'It had everything. Why did it lose?' This question became mine as well, only from the other side: 'What was the combination of intellectual and popular power that gave Christianity the energy lacking in the best of classical philosophical theology?' But this question also assumed an appreciation of the other religions of antiquity, which gave humans access to other aspects of the divine that were erased by Christianity. They too had truths that one could still glimpse, although dimly. I learned no human religious quest is to be simply despised as wrong.

The question about Christianity and classical culture continued to guide my graduate studies, earning a Master's degree in Roman history in 1960 and a PhD in Classics and Patristics in 1965. I also married at this time Herman J. Ruether, a fellow graduate student whose work in political science and Asian studies combined with an interest in the religions of India and Pakistan: Islam,

Hinduism and Buddhism. We had three children between 1958 and 1963 while we were both immersed in our graduate studies. This reality of marriage and children brought me face-to-face with the contradictions of the Catholic views of gender, sexuality and reproduction. I also glimpsed the difficult economics and sociology of trying to be a scholar and mother in our family system and began to write articles on this. This work on family, work and gender would be the germ of a work to be published many years later, *Christianity and the Making of the Modern Family* (2000).

The early 1960s saw also the beginning of the Second Vatican Council and the reform vision that began to sweep through the Church. I wrote several articles critiquing the view of sex and reproduction that underlay the Catholic anti-contraceptive position. One of these became an essay in a book, *Contraception and Holiness*, distributed to the bishops and theologians at the Second Vatican Council. I had become involved in Church politics. Catholic reform has continued to be a deep commitment for me, all the more so when the forces of reaction seem to have 'won' in the twenty-first century. My belief is that, when the 'bad guys' seem to have won, you don't run. You fight harder.

By an extraordinary concatenation of events, the reform movement in the Catholic Church coincided with the civil rights and peace movements in the United States. A second front of trenchant criticism was opening up, questioning the patterns of racism and classism in the United States, as well as its interventionist international policies that brought it into the Vietnam War. In the early 1960s, while I was in graduate studies at Claremont, I was also involved in the ecumenical chaplaincies, which committed themselves to work against racism. In the summer of 1965, they took a delegation to Mississippi as volunteers to work with the Delta Ministry. I was apart of that delegation.

That summer in Mississippi was a crucial turning point in my intellectual development. For the first time I glimpse the United States from the underside, from the perspective of poor, black people in this country, and the face I saw was frightening and dangerous. Our delegation was housed at Beulah, a former black college campus, which was the headquarters of the Delta Ministry. There a variety of projects were underway, including plans for housing and farm cooperatives, voter registration to bring blacks into their full citizen rights and the pre-school education programme 'Mississippi Head Start'.

I committed myself to working with the Head Start programme and travelled through the state, investigating the work of these programmes. We assumed that the local whites hated this work. One night, hooded Klu Klux Klansmen rode through the campus shooting at random at the windows of the buildings. Thereafter we stationed a nightly guard to watch for such incursions and to ring a bell, warning the residents to get under their beds, should such an event occur again. This experience gave me a graphic sense of living in America as a war zone, where one could assume that the local police were one's enemy.

That summer in Mississippi, of seeing America from the underside, brought a social justice focus permanently into my thought. I began to write articles that merged my knowledge of the history of Christian thought with contemporary social issues. Without realizing it, I had hit on a kind of liberation theology. Using a historical method which has guided much of my work since, I asked, 'What are the roots of the issue in Western society and culture?', 'How has Christianity justified this problem?', 'What are the critical traditions in Christian thought that enable us to question this issue?' and, finally, 'How do we go about mobilizing Christian resources to overcome it?'

In 1966, a year after my Mississippi summer, our family moved to Washington, DC, my earlier family home. I took a job at the Howard University School of Religion, a black theological school at a historical black university. I saw this job also as an opportunity to continue my commitment to anti-racism. Black theology and Latin American liberation theology were beginning to be written, and I brought these topics into my classes and writings. When I first came to Howard the term ' black' was still controversial and my middle-class colleagues preferred to call themselves 'negroes'. Thus I found myself in the odd position, as a young white woman, of introducing the writing of Jim Cone and black theology to my mostly African–American, Afro-Caribbean and African students.

Ecology was also an issue that was dawning on the American consciousness. In 1966, I read the Club of Rome report and, for the first time, realized that the present sort of industrial development, which the United States was pursuing and seeking to impose on the rest of the world, was unsustainable. There was no way one could bring the rest of the world into the consumer lifestyle enjoyed by US Americans without destroying the resource base of the planet. Social justice demanded, not a developmentalist expansion of the US system to include others, but a fundamental conversion of this system. My first collection of feminist articles, published in 1975 as *New Woman; New Earth: Sexist Ideologies and Human Liberation*, integrated the ecological issue as its culminating essay. This book has recently been called 'an ecofeminist classic', even though the term 'ecofeminism' had yet to be coined.

In this era of the mid-1960s, race and class analysis was presumed as foundational to critical social thought, but gender was ignored. Neither my black nor my white colleagues in the seminary, or in social activism, thought women's oppression was a worthy subject of discussion. Women with social justice concerns were expected to commit themselves to the liberation of others, not to ask questions about their own exploitation. This began to change dramatically in the late 1960s. Young women in the civil rights movement began to ask questions about 'the place of women in the movement', only to receive the slighting answer from one of its leaders, Stokley Carmichael, that 'the only position of women in the movement is prone'. This 'joke' infuriated the women activists and made clear the combined exploitation of their work and their sexuality, which was taken for granted by male leaders whom they had trusted.

My first talk on sexism and theology, written in 1968, was entitled 'Male Chauvinist Theology and the Anger of Women'. I learned by giving this talk at various seminaries and churches that 'anger' was expected from blacks in response to their discrimination, but taboo for women. In 1972, I was invited to be a visiting scholar at Harvard's Divinity School to teach feminist theology. This gave me a wonderful opportunity to put together research on the historical background of sexism in the Christian traditions from its roots in the ancient Near East to its modern expression and to explore these questions with a bright, critical group of students. Many of them have gone on to be major writers and thinkers in the field.

But sexism was not the only social issue I was exploring in the fall of 1972. Anti-Semitism had long been an area of concern for me. My relation to my uncle David made me aware of and resistant to Christian anti-Judaism as a child. At the end of the Second World War the horror of the Nazi death camps was brought to my nine-year-old consciousness through newsreels. In reading the writings of the Church Fathers I became aware of how often the stereotypes of woman, as representative of the 'bad body', coincided with that of Jews as a different kind of 'bad body'. I began to investigate how Christianity split from Judaism in the first century and forged a polemic against Jews that would be passed down as a heritage of pogroms, until it was taken over by Hitler in the twentieth century in the final pogrom, the Holocaust. I went to Harvard in 1972 to finish a book I had begun to write on Christian anti-Semitism and taught this material that year. It would be published in 1974 as *Faith and Fratricide: The Theological Roots of Anti-Semitism*. None of my feminist or social activist friends understood why I was writing on this topic. They did not see the connection between hatred of Jews and hatred of women and racial groups, such as African–Americans, that seemed so obvious to me.

In 1975, I sensed that my time at Howard School of Religion was coming to an end. Young black women were coming to the seminary and wanted to add the gender issue to the mix of questions, but the faculty was extremely resistant to doing so. One young woman wrote her Master's thesis on sexism in the black church and was openly ridiculed by the faculty. When I tried to defend her I was attacked as 'racist'. It became apparent that this was a no-win situation for a white feminist at a black seminary. It was time for me to move on and to make room for black women professors who could address this issue in the black context. In 1976, I received the offer to be the Georgia Harkness Professor of Applied Theology at Garrett-Evangelical Theological Seminary, a Methodist school on the campus of Northwestern University in Evanston, Illinois that was committed to dealing with both racism and sexism. Our family moved to the Chicago area so I could take this job.

At Garrett I moved to the deepening of many of the issues I had begun to explore from 1966 to 1976. I added to the volume of essays I had published in 1974, *Religion and Sexism: The Image of Women in the Judaeo-Christian Tradition*, a second volume on how women themselves had exercised leadership through the ages: *Women of Spirit: Female Leadership in the Jewish and Christian Traditions* (1978, edited with Eleanor McLaughlin). I began a fruitful collaboration with my colleague at Garrett, Rosemary Skinner Keller, on women and religion in America. Together we would edit the three-volume series, *Women and Religion in America: A Documentary History*, the first volume, on the nineteenth century, published in 1981, the second, on the colonial period, in 1983 and the third, on the first two-thirds of the twentieth century, in 1986. In 1995, we published a synthesis of these three books, together with material from 1965 to the present in the one volume, *In Our Own Voices: Four Centuries of Women's Religious Writings*. Although my own studies had focused on the early centuries of the Church, this work with Rosemary Keller has made me something of an American women's history scholar as well. In the early twenty-first century we are editing together a major two-volume encyclopedia on 'Women and Religion in America', due out in 2004.

My work in feminist theology also resulted in major scholarly ventures. When I first began teaching feminist theology in the early 1980s there were scarcely any resources for such study. Hence, I put together a reader of documents that shows the variety of views of gender in the ancient Near Eastern, Biblical and early Christian traditions, organized around the topics of systematic theology: the nature of God, the trinity, creation, anthropology, Christology, Church, ministry and eschatology. Intentionally, I expanded these readings beyond the Christian tradition, to show resources for looking at gender that existed in the Ancient Near Eastern world into which Judaism was embedded; in Hebrew Scripture, the New Testament, alternative forms of early Christianity found in Gnostics and Montanists, and in modern post-Christian movements, as well as the orthodox tradition.

Using this set of documents I developed a series of lectures that discussed the construction of systematic theology topics from the perspectives of women: for example, asking, 'How had the exclusion of women been justified?' and 'How has this changed over the centuries?' and, finally, 'What are the resources in the tradition for the inclusion of women?' My method involves a double approach: a critique of the exclusionary patterns of theology, but also the lifting up of more inclusionary traditions. The goal of this study is a new construction of the theological theme that is genuinely egalitarian. These lectures were published as *Sexism and Godtalk: Toward a Feminist Theology* (1983, reprint, 1993). The set of readings came out two years later, in 1985 (reprint, 1995), as *Womenguides: Texts for Feminist Theology*.

In 1984, I was offered a Fulbright scholarship to lecture in Sweden. The Swedish women who put together this application for a Fulbright wanted a feminist theologian that could be a resource person for them. I was to give lectures to women in Lund where I was based, and then travel to give additional lectures in Stockholm, Uppsala, Oslo, Copenhagen and Arhus. This was a wonderful opportunity to network with European feminist women in the church and to begin to get a sense of issues in that context. I decided to focus my writing during this period on feminist liturgies and the ecclesiology of 'women church' or feminist base communities, a topic of great interest in the Women-church movement in both America and Europe. This work was published in

1986 as *Women Church: The Theory and Practice of Feminist Liturgical Communities*.

My work on Christian anti-Semitism was also bringing me many opportunities to speak in synagogues and in Jewish–Christian dialogue conferences. Gradually, it became apparent to me that there was an unarticulated political agenda behind many of these invitations. Those Christians critical of Christian anti-Semitism were expected to commit themselves wholeheartedly to the side of the state of Israel in its conflicts with the Palestinians and the Arab world. I was asked questions in the discussion period such as 'Why doesn't the Pope recognize the state of Israel?' Since these questions about the state of Israel had nothing to do with my research or concerns, I was puzzled by such queries. One synagogue mother came up to me after a lecture and whispered to me in a state of great agitation: 'They are just using you.' It became evident that there was a big gap in my understanding of the agenda behind such questions; namely, the politics of American Jews in relation to the state of Israel and the Arab world. I felt I had better learn something about it.

In 1980, I had a chance to travel to Israel with a group of women. The trip was organized by Jewish women from Montreal who billed it as an opportunity for dialogue and peacemaking between women, Jewish, Christian and Muslim. The hope was that somehow women might be able to talk to each other across these differences in ways that men had not. It sounded promising and I signed on. But it soon became evident that the trip was totally skewed on the side of the Israeli–Jewish view of the situation. The one Muslim woman, a Canadian originally from Egypt, dropped out when the bias of the trip became evident. There was no effort to really go to the Palestinian areas or to talk to Palestinians.

I and several other women on the trip, including Charlene Hunter-Galt of the McNeil Lehrer report, began to discuss this bias. We decided to use our free day to 'slip away' from the main itinerary and to meet Palestinians. I knew the writings of Raymonda Tawil, a Palestinian feminist journalist and called her up. She arranged for us to come to their news office in East Jerusalem where we discovered not only Palestinian spokespersons, but critical Israelis of the type to which we had not been exposed on our 'package' tour. Raymonda arranged for us to have a quick exposure to the Palestinian reality by meeting the Mayor of Ramallah (whose legs had been blown off by an Israeli bomb), to visit Palestinian women working in the famed centre, In-ash el-Usra, run by the indomitable Um Khalil (later to run for President of the Palestinian Authority against Yasir Arafat) and to visit a refugee camp.

These brief but intense experiences made us deeply aware of the very different reality that lay just on the other side of the invisible line, the underside of the state of Israel, namely, the dispossessed Palestinians. Our hosts were very upset when we returned, especially with Charlene Hunter-Galt, a prominent African–American journalist whom they had hoped to influence, but they kept their evident anger under control. This intensified our sense that we had uncovered that other story which they had been keeping secret. This deepened my resolve to read about Zionism, the history of Israel and the Palestinian struggle.

In l986, my husband and I took sabbatical leave to live for some months at Tantur, a Christian ecumenical study centre situated on the Bethlehem road, literally at the checkpoint between Israel and Bethlehem. I took the opportunity to teach a class on Zionism, Israel and the Palestinians, while my husband taught on Islam. Our stay at Tantur made us more aware of how religion and the critique of anti-Semitism was being misused to justify the dispossession of the Palestinians, while at the same time ignoring their existence. We came home from the sabbatical with an outline for a book that would cover Christian, Jewish and Islamic views on the land of Palestine and the history of the conflict between Israel and the Palestinians, with an eye to the use and abuse of religious ideology. This was published in 1989 as *The Wrath of Jonah: The Crisis of Religious Nationalism in the Israeli–Palestinian Conflict*.

The publication of this book quickly made evident what we had only suspected, namely, that Jewish–Christian dialogue was predicated on making Christians docile 'yea-sayers' to the policies of the state of Israel, without ever naming the unjust treatment of the Palestinians. I was no longer welcome in Jewish–Christian dialogue conferences and invitations to speak on *Faith and Fratricide* disappeared, even though I had not changed my mind at all about the material in that book. But, at the same time, a new and more rewarding network of colleagues opened up for us, being Christians, Jews and Muslims working on justice for Palestinians.

These networks, such as the Palestinian Human Rights Campaign, gave us an opportunity for many more visits to Israel–Palestine and to edit collections of essays from such conferences, such as *Beyond Occupation: American Jewish, Christian and Palestinian Voices for Peace* (1990) and *Faith and the Intifada: Palestinian Christian Voices* (1992), with Palestinian Christian leader, Naim Ateek and Jewish liberation theologian, Marc Ellis. Marc Ellis was head of the Peace and Justice Center at Maryknoll School of Theology when I first met him in the 1980s. When Maryknoll closed he found himself in a difficult struggle to find another job, given the pressure against him from the American Jewish community in response to the positions he had taken on justice for Palestinians. Finally, he was able to find both a university professorship and the base for a centre on the American Jewish experience at Baylor University in Waco, Texas. The irony that only a Southern Baptist School in Texas was able to risk hiring such a controversial figure, while Christian schools on the East Coast shunned him, was not lost on him or ourselves.

Today the work on Palestinian–Israeli peace and justice and the survival of Palestinian Christians in the 'Holy Land' goes on primarily through the Sabeel Center, a Palestinian liberation theology centre founded by Father Naim Ateek in Jerusalem, with supporting networks in Canada, the United States, Britain and Sweden. But the situation for Palestinians, far from improving in the 1990s with the so-called Oslo 'peace process', greatly worsened. My e-mail news is overwhelmed on a daily basis by stories of the latest random shooting and shelling of Palestinian neighbourhoods by the Israeli army. In the summer of 2001, my husband and I committed ourselves to an update of our book, *The Wrath of Jonah*, to try to capture the main outlines of this worsening history. The gap between the reality of the Palestinian experience and the cover-up of that reality by the dominant media is still very large, and most Americans remain ignorant of the true story.

However intense and absorbing the Palestinian plight, I still remain deeply involved in many other areas of concern. The international feminist movement is a major area of interest for me. Feminism and feminist theology remains myopic if it is confined to white US Americans. Feminist theology must become multicultural, multicontextual. This includes black, Hispanic and Asian feminist theologies in the United States. But of particular interest for me is the development of feminist theologies in Latin America, Africa and Asia. Fortunately, the Ecumenical Association of Third World Theologians, that began to meet in the 1970s to discuss liberation theologies in their various contexts, was willing to expand to support a women's network within this Association.

Women from Latin America, Africa and from many Asian countries began to gather from the mid-1980s to contextualize their women's theologies. I was privileged to be able to go to some of the international meetings of First and Third World women's theologies, as well as to travel to many Latin American countries; to the African countries of South Africa and Zimbabwe and to China, Japan, Korea, the Philippines and India to meet and work with women in these many contexts. In 1996, I published a book of essays that featured the ecofeminist work of women across these three continents in *Women Healing Earth: Third World Women on Feminism, Religion and Ecology*. I also give a synopsis of the theological work emerging from such 'Third World' women in the last chapter of my 1998 book, *Women and Redemption*.

The intersection of feminism and ecology had already been suggested in my 1975 book, *New Woman, New Earth*. In 1992, I published a volume that is explicitly ecofeminist, showing how the domination of women and of the 'earth' has been deeply interconnected in Christianity: *Gaia and God: An Ecofeminist Theology of Earth Healing*. This concern became central to my writings in the 1990s and also brought me into contact with people like Mary Evelyn Tucker of Bucknell University who was interested in exploring ecological resources in the many world religions. In 1999, Mary Evelyn was able to help direct a series of conferences through the Harvard Center for World Religions on ecological resources in ten world religions. I spoke and became the editor of the Christian volume of this series, together with Dieter Hessal, a long time worker on theological education and ecology (*Christianity and Ecology*, 2000).

Ecumenism and dialogue between world religions has long been an interest of mine, but I saw myself as limited to the religions of the West, Judaism, Christianity and Islam. I did not see myself becoming a student of Asian religions, and turned to my husband, Herman Ruether, for occasional resources on this topic. However, in the mid-1980s, my old teacher from Claremont, John Cobb, recruited me to join the Buddhist–Christian dialogue group that he had founded with Japanese Buddhist, Maseo Abe. Protesting that I was already 'spread too thin', I eventually agreed to join, primarily motivated by the evident need to bring feminist perspectives into this dialogue. There I found friend and colleague Rita Gross seeking to articulate the Buddhist side of the feminist issue.

Rita and I began to engage in collaborative work, doing joint presentations on Christian and Buddhist feminist critique of our religions for the Cobb–Abe dialogue group. In the fall of 1999, we did a joint workshop on this topic at the Christian Center of the Grail. We traced our own autobiographical root into the dialogue, what we found liberating and what we found oppressive in our traditions and what each of us found helpful for ecological concerns. It quickly became apparent that we had a book from these joint lectures. We would not only write more fully on the main topics of our dialogue, but also do a short response to each other's lectures. This dialogue was published in the spring of 2001 as *Religious Feminism and the Future of the Planet: A Buddhist–Christian Conversation*.

2001 saw a major change in my life. I retired, after 26 years, from Garrett-Evangelical Theological Seminary, to move to California to be the Carpenter Professor of Feminist Theology at the Graduate Theological Union in Berkeley. For me, return to California is a return home in many ways. It is a place of old family roots of my mother's family (since 1846).

This move is a chance to take stock of my intellectual development and writings over the last 35 years. Will I continue to write on these same topics? I expect I will. None of ecology, feminism or the Palestinian situation shows any sign of losing its edge in the next decade or two. I envision doing a feminist–womanist dialogue book with an African–American womanist theologian some time in the future. I would like to do something on American liberation theology, evaluating where Third World liberation theology is today, and how US Americans, so often and rightly the butt of its criticism, need to respond to it. Questions include: 'Can we release our hold on dominating power over others and transform ourselves into one nation among others in a just, peaceful and ecologically sustainable world?'; 'What is the mind-set that ties the United States with the imperial obsession to be "Number 1, militarily and economically"?', and finally, 'What are the resources in our religious culture for "letting go" of this obsession?'

My theological writings remain deeply tied to the disciplines in which I was trained at Scripps College and Claremont Graduate School in 1954–65, being the history of ideas in their social context. But this trajectory of research is, at the same time, advocacy scholarship. It is about helping us (Christians, US Americans) understand how we got into the horrible distortions of anti-Semitism, racism, sexism, international militarism, imperialism and ecological devastation so that we can begin to imagine how we can get out of them. My theological work not only helps our understanding but also examines what resources we have in our traditions and in those symbols that form the basis for the best of our identity and which help us transcend systems and ideologies of oppression in order to glimpse a better world of partnership with each other and with the earth. These partnerships might, at the same time, help us glimpse a more life-giving relation to God.

Chapter 10

How I Changed My Mind

Kathryn Tanner

When I was in graduate school at Yale in the early 1980s (working primarily with Hans Frei, George Lindbeck and Louis Dupré), the main worries of both theologians and philosophers of religion were methodological in nature: to justify religious thought, either by showing how it met the usual standards of meaning, intelligibility and truth endorsed by other disciplines, or (the preferred tactic of Frei and Lindbeck) by showing, with an ironic display of academic rigour, why no such effort of justification was necessary. Epistemological issues (such as how meaning and truth were conveyed linguistically through signs and symbols) and biblical hermeneutics were the bread and butter of our studies. Methodological preoccupations were what distinguished theological schools (Yale and the University of Chicago), and these fights were formulated as a continuation of controversies within neo-orthodoxy and Karl Barth (our hero), on the one hand, versus Rudolf Bultmann and Paul Tillich, on the other. The history of Christian thought, another main focus of our study, was taught with these same methodological emphases in mind.

My teachers, Frei and Lindbeck, often half-jokingly quipped that one day they would eventually *do* theology, rather than spend all their time talking about how to go about it; but neither of them, as it turns out, made it to that point in their own work. Nowadays, however, their hopes (at least in this regard) have come to fruition in the new generation of US theologians, who (whatever their methodological backgrounds or proclivities) dare to say something as 'constructive' theologians, reworking Christian themes to address the challenges of today's world. Pick up almost any work in theology today and you are liable to find a discussion of the Trinity and its implications for politics, or a reformulation of God's relation to creation as an impetus to ecological responsibility, or a rethinking of the atonement in light of trauma theory. Frei, my old friend, at once so cautious and generous, would no doubt be astounded and grateful; and perhaps a little envious too, pleasantly surprised but concerned for the brazen boldness of it all.

This shift from methodological to substantive preoccupations is partly a response to, and incorporation of, the lessons of liberation theology, which effectively undercut the Enlightenment as the taken-for-granted starting point for theological work. The need is not so much to show the meaningfulness of Christianity in today's world but rather what Christianity can contribute to making the world a better place. The same sort of shift is also encouraged by post-modern trends in academic disciplines. With the onset of a post-modern humility about pretensions to such things as universality and disinterestedness, the particularism of specifically Christian sources of insight and the advocacy stance assumed by many theologians are far less suspect than they used to be. The theoretical deficiencies of which theology has been accused are now so spread around that they appear to be the defining fault of no one field in particular, and significant differences among fields in this regard seem mere matters of degree. The legitimacy of theology, to the extent it remains a question in American intellectual life, is no longer a matter of whether theology can meet some scholarly minimum in its procedures. Theology's warrant now centres on the question of whether theologians have anything important to say about the world and our place in it. What, if anything, can the Christian theologian positively contribute to the search for the true and the right on particular issues of importance in the twenty-first century? What resources does the Christian symbol system provide for resolving such issues? How might that symbol system be creatively recast in the process?

Answers to these questions require new methods. Theology's closest analogue is no longer a perennial philosophy, addressing the most general questions of human moment purportedly common to every time and place, but a political theory (broadly construed) of cultural meanings that is quite situation-specific in its focus. In other words, the theologian – like a Weberian social scientist or a Gramscian political theorist – now asks about the way Christian beliefs and symbols function in the particulars of people's lives so as to direct and justify the shape of social organization and the course of social action. As a historian of Christian thought and practice, the theologian needs a thorough knowledge of the way these intersections of culture and politics have panned out across differences of time and place: a thorough knowledge of the various permutations of the Christian symbol in all its complicated alignments with social forces for good or ill. With this knowledge in hand, the constructive theologian is better positioned to intervene in the current situation adroitly, effectively and responsibly, with suggestions for both rethinking Christian claims and refiguring human life for the sake of the greater good.

My own theological trajectory has followed this outline. I initially turned to theology from philosophy, which in my day at Yale as an undergraduate involved (unusually for the time) the broad study of both continental and analytic philosophy, and familiarity with American pragmatism and process thought. The linguistic turn had been made, deconstruction was in the air, Thomas Kuhn had initiated a sociology of knowledge that chastened the objectivist ideal of science as a paradigm for all other disciplines; but the blurring of philosophy into anthropology and literary theory – now so common – had yet to take hold. Theology held for me the hope of addressing questions of meaning in a comprehensive fashion that philosophers themselves now seemed reluctant to pursue. Theology as a form of intellectual inquiry was clearly about something (not talk about talk about talk) and offered direction and significance to the pursuit of the true and the right through a community of inquiry outside itself – the Church. Theology, in short, seemed to matter to 'someone'. Under the impact of post-liberalism, which had just begun to solidify around the work of Frei and Lindbeck during my time in graduate school, my work has increasingly made that community of inquiry (religious people in their efforts to forge a way of life) its focus as both subject matter and object for intervention with a corresponding broadening of methods, away from philosophy as traditionally construed.

My first book, *God and Creation in Christian Theology* (1988), was a wide-ranging analysis of patterns of discourse about God and creation in Christian thought. It discussed the way such patterns of discourse modified habits of speech in the wider society in order to show (rather than explain) the coherence of various Christian claims about God and the world; and discussed how those patterns of discourse were distorted and coherence was lost, under modern strain. Because Christian language was never adequate to the God to which it referred, the theologian was concerned, not directly with that referent, but with the habits of speech and action that amounted to God's direction of Christian lives. Intellectual difficulties arising out of everyday Christian practice (for example, the inability to resolve how I am to be responsible for the character of my life while dependent, nevertheless, on God's grace) set off theological questions about the compatibility of asserting both human and divine responsibility for our actions; and those questions were resolved by altering the way we usually speak of action in common.

My next book, *The Politics of God* (1992), moved to a more overt discussion of the function of religious discourse in Christian lives by exploring how beliefs about God and creation shaped the political stances of Christians. Discourse in an analytic mode, the method of the first book, was insufficient here; the method was now something closer to that of sociology or anthropology. This book did not simply describe Christian practice (while commending it for its coherence, as the first book did). It argued a normative case, how beliefs about God and creation *should* shape Christian lives, in self-conscious opposition to the way those beliefs have commonly functioned to ill effect in the past and present. The next book, *Theories of Culture: A New Agenda for Theology* (1997), raised this new method up as the primary subject for discussion. The latest, *Jesus, Humanity and the Trinity: A Brief Systematic Theology* (2001), ventures a clear vision of the whole 'Christian thing' (as David Kelsey, another of my Yale teachers, would put it) – Trinity, creation, covenant, Christology and eschatology, all oriented towards the idea of God as gift giver – in order to establish a consistent Christian outlook on life and the corresponding character of human responsibilities.

Despite the idiosyncrasies of my own trajectory, this constructive focus on Christianity as a world-view and orienting point for social action, and the way it brings theologians into conversation with social scientists, is, I have said, not particularly unusual on the present scene: liberation, African–American and feminist theologies, historicist and pragmatist-influenced theologies, theologies originating in a Tillichian brand of correlation, are often found moving in these same directions. One thing that sets my own efforts apart is the place of historical study for a creative reworking of Christian ideas and symbols to meet present challenges.

Relevant in this connection is the fact that one of the things that originally attracted me to theology was its oddity in the secular university and on the contemporary scene (despite the characteristically modern rise of fundamentalism as a world historical force). Theology had the ability to propose the unexpected, to shock and startle. It offered an escape from the taken-for-granted certainties of life, by referring them to something that remained ever beyond them, resisting capture and encapsulation. The theologian respects that capacity, it seems to me, not by dressing up contemporary commonplaces in religious terms, but in seeking what lies beyond a contemporary outlook and beyond the immediate context of one's work. A theology that starts from, and uses as its toolbox for creative ends, materials gathered from the widest possible purview is, in my opinion, a theology with that imaginative expansiveness. Such a theology looks to the Christian past not for models for simple imitation but for a way to complicate one's sense of the possibilities for present Christian expression and action. It looks to the past not to restrict and cramp what might be said now but to break out of the narrowness of a contemporary sense of the realistic. It complements an understanding of the complex variety of pre-modern theologies in the West with an understanding of the complex forms of Christianity's global reach now and in the past. It reaches beyond the narrowness of denominational confines to the broadest ecumenical vision, and sees beyond elite forms of theological expression, primarily in written texts, to the popular theologies of everyday life.

All of that is what I mean by a 'constructive' theology that is historically funded: the pre-modern, the popular, the global and the ecumenical put to use to shake up, reorient and expand what one would have thought one could do with the Christian symbol system, in the constructive effort to figure out the proper Christian stance for today's world.

The breadth of this understanding of the historical, and the focus here on the historical complexity and variability of Christian forms of life, indicate ways that I have moved beyond my Yale training, where the talk was commonly of *the* biblical world and *the* Christian tradition. I have also done so in refusing to understand Christian ways of living in isolation from the wider culture. Christian ways of speaking and acting are not created out of whole cloth but are constituted by odd modifications to ways of speaking and acting that are current in the wider society. It is therefore impossible to understand their meaning and social point without understanding the culture of the wider society and what Christian habits of speech and action are saying about it through modifications made to it. For example, when Christians call Jesus 'Lord' that is a comment on the Lords of the wider society which is impossible to understand without knowing what is unusual about that attribution in the context of its use; for example, contrary to its usual application, 'Lord' in Christian uses refers to a person shamefully crucified like a criminal and enemy of the state. Similarly, the significance of eating in church is not clear until one understands the eating practices of the wider society, modifications to those practices in church becoming a kind of commentary on them (for example, a criticism of the exclusions of ordinary table fellowship).

Theological construction, figuring out what it is that Christians should 'say' and 'do' in one's present context, therefore requires a highly complicated and subtle reading of the whole cultural field into which Christianity figures. One is helped here again by historical analysis (in my broad sense) that incorporates such a holistic cultural perspective. Theology is always a matter of judgments regarding the practices of the wider society and about the degree and manner in which they should also figure in Christian lives. Knowledge of how Christians have made such judgments at other times and places, and one's own sense, in hindsight or at a distance, about whether they did so correctly, in suitably Christian fashion, provide invaluable insights and practice in tackling the issues of one's own time and circumstance when the personal stakes are much higher.

Method, I have learned, is not a safeguard for such judgment. Karl Barth was shocked by his teachers' support for the First World War into a rejection of the method of Protestant liberalism. But I have been shocked by many of my American theological colleagues' responses to the political upsurge of the Christian right in the United States, and the present culture wars here, into the sense that method (as it has been traditionally conceived) is not sufficient. Too many of my teachers (and here I mean 'teachers' very broadly as those already established on the theologian scene and from whom I therefore expected wisdom and guidance) read, it seemed to me, the upsurge of the religious right simply as a salutary entrance of religion into the public square, promising an elevation in the seriousness with which theological exchange would have to be taken from now on by the wider society. *What* the religious right was promulgating was of less interest to them. Shame at the fact that Christianity stood so publicly for *this* was not, as far as I could see, at a premium. Given the at least superficial similarities between the post-liberalism of my immediate circle of teachers and that of the religious right (for example, preoccupation with the world of the Bible, repudiation of apologetics and a stance in opposition to liberal culture), the failure of post-liberal theologians to criticize the right could easily be taken for an endorsement. So that silence not be taken for praise, the situation required, it seemed to me, only the most forceful repudiation of the right's political judgments, something that I tried to do, in my own limited way, in *The Politics of God*. The post-liberal reluctance to be more than a witness to the wider society had to be overcome. It seemed to me, instead, that one's sense of that witness itself was to be formed in direct engagement with the political developments of the day.

What I carry away from this time (which unfortunately is not over) is the belief that it is misguided to search for proper theological method with the expectation that it will make clear, all by itself, the proper Christian stance on the contested sociocultural issues of one's day. Search for proper method with that expectation encourages blanket judgments about the wider culture as a whole – it is to be resisted, or welcomed as the ground floor for the contributions of grace, or transformed as a whole – when what is really necessary is an often more difficult and nuanced discernment about particulars.

Advocating either the Word as norm for Christian judgment with Barth or critical correlation with Tillich does not help very much when the question is how to read the situation in a Christian light. What, for example, does feminism or the movement for gay liberation represent in Christian terms? An instance of moral irresponsibility which Christians should resist or an intent to further full human flourishing to which Christians should be sympathetic? Such judgments have much more to do with the substantive character of one's understanding of what Christianity is all about than they do with the method used to come up with it. To make a simplistic parallel with Barth again, Christians supported the Nazis not because they neglected the Word in favour of cultural trends but because they had a misguided understanding of Christianity. Hitler's National Socialism was wrong on a Christian understanding of things because its policy towards Jews (and others) was un-Christian and not because it forced the neglect of the Word by making the nation-state all. Clearly, a nation-state could respect the Word and persecute Jews, depending on its understanding of what Christianity was all about, and that would merit as grave a theological condemnation as any the Barmen Declaration offered. Christians are always influenced, one way or another, by the cultural trends of the day and respect for the Word does not exempt them from its effects (as Barth himself recognized in *Church Dogmatics*, I/2).

It is what Christians do with those influences that matters, as they grow into an understanding of their Christian commitments by way of complex processes of revision, appropriation and resistance to those cultural trends, taken one by one. One never rejects everything, since one's Christianity always remains parasitic to some extent on the wider society's forms of life. Nor (one hopes) does one accept everything, because Christian justifications even for courses of action shared with the wider society alter their sense and point. One's judgments about different aspects of the wider society's practices need not, moreover, be the same. For example, my grave worries about economic inequalities that are the product of global capitalism need not spill over onto the greater economic opportunities for women that are also a feature of recent economic developments in the West. An equal resistance to both, simply because they are the 'world' that Christianity is to reject, leads to dishonesty about the way that the world inevitably figures in even the best Christian lives, and to a lazy reneging on Christian responsibilities to judge particulars with care.

As I have argued in *Theories of Culture*, I think that theologians have to be honest about the complexities of Christian lives and the way Christian beliefs and symbols figure there. Doing so means taking seriously what disciplines such as sociology and anthropology reveal: the often messy, ambiguous and porous character of the effort to live Christianly. Trained historians of Christianity – particularly historians who also avail themselves of the insights of these other disciplines – were not surprised by my methodological recommendation in that book. Theologians, commonly in my experience, have yet to make the leap.

Chapter 11

A Constructive Contemporary Theology

Keith Ward

I was born in a rural area of Northern England at the beginning of the Second World War. My upbringing and education was almost wholly non-religious, although religion was seen as an option that was available for those who liked it. I myself participated in Anglican and Methodist worship, and encountered a number of esoteric schools, like that of Rudolf Steiner and the Rosicrucians. So I had a very clear sense from an early age that there were a wide variety of religious opinions, and that religion as such was a minority interest. More important was the gaining of knowledge about the natural world in the sciences, the pursuit of culture in music and the arts, and the love of nature.

I became a Christian as a result of personal experience, which, as I recall it, was primarily an experience of the living presence of Christ, or of the Spirit of God (not clearly distinguished), as an energizing and inspiring power inwardly known. There was little doctrine involved in this. Indeed, I was unaware of the major Christian doctrines of the Trinity, Incarnation and Atonement for quite a number of years. I was always encouraged to be eclectic and wide-ranging in my reading, so I read Radhakrishnan before I read any Christian theologian, and I probably knew more about Indian religions and esoteric traditions like Anthroposophy (from books) than I did about the Christian faith, theoretically speaking. But I had no doubt that I experienced a spiritual presence which had become known to me through the various very different, but always Protestant, Christian communities I encountered. Catholicism and Conservative Evangelical Protestantism were never parts of my early experience.

I would say, looking back, that I had a real, vivid, experiential but doctrinally vague, religious faith. At a slightly later stage I did encounter Evangelical Christians, and was vastly impressed by their commitment and their deep experience of Christ, which certainly renewed my own faith. I also encountered Catholicism, and was again impressed by the beauty of the liturgy and the appealingly 'mystical' approach I found there. But I was never convinced of the intellectual plausibility of many of the beliefs I encountered in these traditions, which seemed to me as I was told them often both rather myopic and unduly restrictive. People just seemed to be remarkably ill-informed about what the various religious traditions of the world said, though that did not seem to stop them knowing such traditions were wrong!

So part of the context of my development was the growing awareness of the many world-views, religious and non-religious, which during my early life were becoming much better known in Britain, and the consequential awareness that Christian beliefs were not at all obviously true or even rational to many people. At that time, many hitherto inaccessible works in Indian and Chinese philosophy were being translated, and scholars from Eastern traditions were coming to Britain to expound their faiths in their own way. So there was a vast increase in the possibilities of reading the primary texts of the world religions in translation, and of discussing their contents with scholars in those religions. There was no longer any excuse for confining one's religious knowledge to just one Western version of Christianity.

When I went to university, after some vacillation I studied philosophy. The dominant school of thought was what is often called 'linguistic analysis'. It concentrated on analysing the meaning of words, especially difficult words like 'beauty', 'goodness' and 'God'. And it was usually pretty insistent that all words that claimed factual content had to be rooted in realities that were observable by means of the senses. Two of the most influential philosophers when I was a student were A.J. Ayer and Gilbert Ryle (who was my tutor). Ayer was particularly vehement in his rejection of religion as based on meaningless terms or empty hypotheses. Ryle was more disinterested, assuming that religious beliefs were either relics of primitive superstition or expressions of emotional needs. Even philosophers who were religious were very muted in the claims they made. Ian Ramsey, the Nolloth Professor of the Philosophy of the Christian Religion, had a great influence on me. He sometimes described himself as a 'religious empiricist'. His view was that the term 'God' was used to mark moments of disclosure, when one discerned the empirical facts and 'more', but a 'more' that could only be expressed in symbol and metaphor. Religion was not about belief in mighty acts of God that broke the laws of nature. It was not about abstract metaphysical dogmas, which could establish truths about a creator of the world by reason. It was basically about total life commitments that arose from discernments of a transcendent dimension in experience.

When I came to the study of theology, it was with this academic background. So it was not surprising that the language of Karl Barth seemed to come as if from some alien universe, where people were not concerned with clarity or with the precise analysis of the meanings of the terms they used. The language of Paul Tillich was redolent of the grand metaphysical systems of Hegel and the idealists, whose pretensions had been deflated simply by asking precisely what they meant. And many theologians, where they were interested in doctrines, were still involved in fourth- and fifth-century debates about ancient Greek philosophical terms (or, if Catholic, in thirteenth-century neo-Aristotelian terms) which again belonged to a past philosophical landscape. My problem was to avoid the solvent acids of philosophical atheism, while preserving the positive goods of definitional clarity, analytical precision, logical rigour and insistence on reasoned justification, which linguistic philosophy had established, at least in the academic world of philosophy.

Another important factor was the amazing development in the sciences during my lifetime. I was always fascinated by science, especially by physics. The discovery of nuclear fission, the development of quantum mechanics, the unravelling of the structure of DNA, and the development of computing, are just four of the world-changing scientific breakthroughs that have happened within my lifetime. Religion makes bold statements about the ultimate nature of reality, and new physics, biology and information technology provide new information about at least the ultimate nature of physical reality. This leaves believers with the problem of how to relate traditional beliefs, formulated entirely in pre-scientific cultures, to these amazing new discoveries about the nature and history of the physical universe. It is wise for people like me to tread delicately in these areas, which grow more complex and refined by the day. But it seems to me an abrogation of responsibility for anyone interested in the truth of basic religious doctrines to ignore this new information.

I was encouraged enormously as I tried to face up to the problems raised by philosophical criticism of religion and by new scientific advances by meeting a number of theologians who were well aware of the problems and were engaged in developing responses to them. Ian Ramsey, John Robinson, Geoffrey Lampe, Arthur Peacocke, Maurice Wiles and John Macquarrie are perhaps the best known of those who influenced my thought. To some people, this may seem like a litany of sceptics, and I did try from time to time to defend a more robustly traditional faith than they seemed to have. But I increasingly came to feel that they embodied both the virtues of critical enquiry and width of vision, and of commitment to the God they discerned in and through the person of Jesus, which I found it hard to discover anywhere else. This might only be one strand of Christian faith, but it did exist as an important part of twentieth-century British religious thought, and it was one I could affirm.

It was slightly surprising to me that many of these thinkers did not seriously consider religions in general, though of course one cannot do everything in one lifetime. It seemed to me, though, that the sort of interpretation they gave to Christian faith was equally applicable to many elements of religious life throughout the world. As I read the works of A.C. Bouquet, John Hick, Wilfred Cantwell Smith and Ninian Smart, I began to gain some idea of the way in which the diverse religious traditions of humanity might fit into a broad pattern that was coherent and intelligible. Henceforth, I came to feel Christianity could only be properly understood in its global context, as one element of a broad pattern of faiths, rooted in the diverse but interlinked histories of human cultures.

For most of my academic life I have taught in Departments of Philosophy, but since my ordination in 1972 as an Anglican priest I have worked in local parishes as a non-stipendiary priest, and I have always been primarily interested in religious questions. Eventually, I gave in to the inevitable, and became a theologian and even, completely to my surprise, a canon of Christ Church in Oxford.

What I suppose is my major work is a four-volume *Comparative Theology*, which brings together the three main themes that have dominated my intellectual life: an interest in global religions, an interest in a philosophical approach to religious beliefs and an interest in the sciences. It seeks to present a systematic Christian theology in the context of the development of religion globally, and to bring out both its distinctive insights and its peculiar limitations. It also seeks to explore a number of main pathways that religious commitment has taken throughout the world, in as sensitive and yet critical a way as possible. It is comparative, because it compares and contrasts, in a broadly descriptive way, various religious beliefs about revelation, God, human nature and the right way to live. It is theological, because it is concerned with issues of rationality and truth. Thus it is normative, providing constructive suggestions about how to understand one particular faith tradition in a rationally justifiable way.

I have discovered that there have been two major misunderstandings of what that work was doing. One is that I was from the first a Christian apologist, using or misusing ideas from other faiths, taken out of context, to demonstrate the superiority of my own. The other misunderstanding is that I was claiming to stand outside religions and judge them all from some better standpoint, or to advocate some new global religions that would supersede all present faiths. I am comforted by the fact that these criticisms accuse me of opposite tendencies, which makes me think that at least they cannot both be fair. In fact I did write from a particular Christian viewpoint, looking for insights from other faiths and trying to present my own views persuasively, though in full awareness that believers in other faiths would be expected to do just the same thing from their own different viewpoints. And though my approach to Christianity may be regarded as revisionist in some ways, it is certainly not one that tries to supersede Christianity or any other faith, and to propose some superior form of religion. My aim was, in short, to be descriptively fair to all faiths, and prescriptively reasonable in showing how one form of Christian faith could be justifiably maintained in face of so many competing world-views.

Some of the main results of my enquiry were the following. First, all faiths were subject to the same sorts of internal diversities, tensions and ambiguities that are familiar in Christianity. Second, in the last 200 years Christianity had, rather painfully, come to accept critical attitudes to Scripture and to authority as part of its complex being in the world. All traditions will, I think, have to face such criticism sooner or later. Third, I turned out (and this surprised me in some ways) to belong pretty squarely in a theological tradition that probably begins with Schleiermacher early in the nineteenth century and that, while still controversial, has continued as an important strand of Christian theology ever since. Fourth, I concluded that some central beliefs about God and the spiritual life were held in common by the major religious traditions, but were expressed in different cultural and historical symbols, deriving from different histories and background views of the world. Fifth, I was confirmed in my suspicion that Christianity itself had changed fairly radically, and more than once, from its first beginnings in Galilee, and that it is actually part of its inner nature to continue to have possibilities of development in new self-transformations in relation to new moral and factual insights.

The upshot of all this has been to confirm me in what I fully recognize to be just one strand of Christian believing, but to make me feel that it is vitally important to learn to understand and respect all that is good in other conscientiously formulated traditions, both Christian and non-Christian. I believe that the most basic and fundamental religious belief is, in a rather vague but still important sense, agreed in most of the religious traditions of which I am aware. This is that there is a spiritual realm which is in some sense more real than, and probably the basis of, the material world. There are many ways of construing and representing this realm, but there develops in most traditions the idea of one being or state of supreme value, which it is possible to apprehend in some form. Furthermore, the way to that apprehension is a way of overcoming egoism, pride and hatred, so as to let that spiritual reality be expressed in one's own life. The religious life is one of seeking to apprehend the supreme value and let it be manifest in human life, in face of a constant human tendency to egoism and hatred. This belief and commitment has been worked out in various ways in human history, and part of a broader spiritual understanding is to appreciate the history of humanity's religious search in all its incompleteness and ambiguity.

As I see it, the distinctiveness of Christian faith is that it sees the paradigm revelation as given in the life, death and resurrection of Jesus, who is the historical and personal form of God on this planet. It sees God as a being of limitless and universal love. It sees human lives as trapped in bondage to desire, pride and hatred, but also as liberated and united to God through the inner action of the Spirit of God. It sees the Church, the many communities of the followers of Christ, as called to the vocation of proclaiming the good news of liberation and eternal life, and of serving the world in love. It sees the ultimate destiny of human life, and in some sense of the whole cosmos, as being taken up into the life of God, where all evil is redeemed and all good is conserved forever.

My approach in theology has been to try to work out how this form of contemporary Christianity can formulate its own distinctive approach in the light of the many intellectual and moral criticisms of religion in post eighteenth-century Europe, of the increased possibility of understanding religious traditions in a global way, and of the new world-view which the sciences are opening up to us. The theology that results is perhaps more tentative, questioning and consciously provisional than some would like. But I think it is compatible with a commitment to that passionate love of God, as discerned in Jesus Christ, which is central to Christian faith. Living in faith, and living with uncertainty, are, after all, not so very far removed from one another.

Chapter 12

Discovering Dogmatics

John Webster

I

Humanly speaking, I became a theologian largely by accident. Having specialized in languages and literature at school, I went to Cambridge to read English, with the hope of getting to grips with comparative literature and the history of ideas. After a couple of disappointing terms, increasingly frustrated with what I thought of as the myopia of practical criticism detached from literature as a moral practice, I changed to study theology. Though I chose theology only because I could not think of anything else I wanted to do, I was quickly engrossed. Partly, that was because theological study set before me an immense store of texts, concepts and language of extraordinary power, a whole imaginative and intellectual world; partly, again, it was because that store helped me to articulate in a rudimentary way and for the first time convictions which had been deeply important but inchoate since my conversion from watery suburban Methodism into a tough version of Calvinistic Christianity.

My interests were drawn to systematic and modern historical theology, and when I stayed on for graduate work, that became my focus. In the late 1970s, systematic theology was still somewhat marginal in Cambridge theology, as it was in English theology as a whole (with some notable exceptions). Christian doctrine was chiefly taught through analysis of *problems*, particularly the problems faced by those who felt acutely responsible to do their theology under the bleak searchlights of what were taken to be normative modern intellectual developments. Dominating the curriculum as it did, this approach – roughly speaking, it can be called 'doctrinal criticism' – had a suppressive effect on constructive theology, for a number of reasons. It tended to fragment the corpus of Christian doctrine, isolating individual theological loci and underplaying or even ignoring the interconnectedness of the whole (I was, for example, never offered a course of lectures on the major topics of systematic theology, and none of my teachers ever wrote an overall account of Christian doctrine, preferring instead the kind of critical dissection of one or other problematic bit as exemplified in a standard book from the period in Geoffrey Lampe's *God as Spirit*). It tended, further, to be heavily preoccupied with issues of theological method (hermeneutics, pluralism in theology, theology and historical science, the nature of religious language), anxiously defining and redefining its relationship to the sources of theology, yet curiously inhibited in making much use of them. And it tended to lack a robust sense of its own integrity and coherence as a field of intellectual inquiry, and so to expend a great deal of energy in forming alliances with other disciplines (principally philosophy and history, but sometimes social theory or philosophy of natural science) as a means of reassurance.

All of this meant that neither undergraduate theological study nor graduate work gave me much by way of doctrinal formation; I was well schooled in the tactics of criticism, but not taught how to inhabit and think from a tradition. There were compensations: a *Doktorvater* who set me to read the classics of modern German Protestant divinity; the presence in the Faculty of the great troubled genius of Donald MacKinnon, who regarded dogmatics with utter seriousness and growled at anyone who did not; a thesis topic (Jüngel, at that time an exotic mix of Luther, Heidegger and Barth) which not only forced me to look at some major issues in Christian doctrine but also led me to busy myself with the writings of the grand old man of Basel.

After graduate work, I found a job teaching systematic theology in a Church of England theological college in the North East of England. In retrospect, I was desperately ill-prepared, lacking a mature sense of the scope of Christian doctrine, pretty ignorant about much of its history, and more than anything else still needing to break free of the habit of going straight to critical questions. Moreover, I had yet to clarify satisfactorily the task of Christian doctrine, its relation to exegesis and its role in the life of the Church. As a result, when I look back on what I taught and wrote at that time, it seems to me to lack the right sort of clarity, focus and coherence that can only be derived from a sense of the vocation of theological work.

That vocation only began to clarify itself for me when I moved to teach in a large ecumenical federation of seminaries in Canada. No longer responsible for undergraduate instruction, I was free to specialize in my work and to pursue matters at much greater depth than had hitherto been possible. More particularly, I learned the art of running a text seminar (something to which my own studies had never exposed me), and spent a good deal of labour inching my way through classic and contemporary texts with groups of graduate students. Gradually, I began to find my way out of doctrinal criticism, to realize that its scruples were in large measure misplaced, and so to rediscover that positive Christian dogmatics is a wise, edifying and joyful science.

A number of things came together to extract me from the inhibitions of my theological formation. One very prominent factor was a half-conscious but remarkably emancipating decision to teach confessionally, in two senses. First, I resolved to work on the assumption of the truthfulness and helpfulness of the Christian confession, and not to devote too much time and energy developing arguments in its favour or responses to its critical denials. I discovered, in other words, that description is a great deal more interesting and persuasive than apology. Second, I resolved to structure the content of my teaching in accordance with the intellectual and spiritual logic of the Christian confession as it finds expression in the classical creeds, to allow that structure to stand and to explicate itself, and not to press the material into some other format. Thus my survey of Christian doctrine was (and remains) simply a conceptual expansion of the Apostles' Creed as a guide to the Gospel that is set out in Holy Scripture. Once I resolved to work in this way, I quite quickly found that the substance and order of Christian doctrine displayed itself as much more grand, and much more comprehensible, than when I had approached it as a series of critical problems.

A second factor was exposure to different theological and ecclesial traditions, and especially to Roman Catholicism, in an ecumenical school. In part, this meant encountering others engaged in theological work who had experienced much more profound (often French or German) theological formation and whose arrangement of the doctrinal substance of the Christian faith made me more acutely aware of my own preferences. But it was also a matter of coming to see that the real fault-lines do not necessarily run between the denominations but across them; that is, it slowly dawned on me that the critical divergences are not those between Roman Catholic and Protestant, but the divergence between those who think that the classical exegetical and dogmatic tasks of theology are no longer viable in an historical age, and those who are unpersuaded of the need to abandon those tasks.

In this respect, I was exceedingly fortunate to have as a close colleague and fellow teacher a Jesuit philosophical theologian and historian of modern theological thought. In endless discussions he helped me transform my instincts about the unfruitfulness of doctrinal criticism into a more lucid critique of the career of modern Christian divinity. He did so in a couple of ways. First, by a series of stringently critical readings of some major modern philosophical and theological texts he made explicit some of the most important precepts of modernity (about interiority, experience, instrumental rationality, the priority of the natural over the positive, the necessity of foundations) and displayed how they could be seen in operation in contemporary theological writing. His target was often North American revisionist and correlationist theology, especially its Roman Catholic variants, but most of the same critical conclusions could readily be reached about Protestant theology, and especially about the sort of theological style from which I was detaching myself. Second, and for me more crucially, he argued that the expansion of the prestige of critical philosophy in modern theology was partly to be explained by the steady retraction of Christian doctrine. That is, the explanatory success of critical philosophy depended upon the incapacity of Church and theology to deploy doctrinal and exegetical material to meet its challenges. Rather than appealing to its own theological and spiritual substance, Christian theology had frequently tried to meet its challengers on their own ground, and thereby often robbed itself of the very arguments which it should have mounted in its defence. Taken together, these two lessons finally shook me free from the vestiges of doctrinal criticism, which I could then set in perspective as a late (and not particularly noble) expression of theological idealism which I no longer found compelling.

My Jesuit colleague was Yale-trained: suspicious of the generic, deeply interested in the role of the communal aspects of human knowledge and practice, concerned for the recovery of the plain sense of Scripture over and against the Romantic hermeneutics of presence. Like others in the late 1980s who were searching, dissatisfied both with theological liberalism and with merely reactionary agendas, and for a constructive way forward in theology, I was much preoccupied with the theological work that came out of Yale. In part, this was because that work was often undertaken in defiance of revisionist proprieties; but it was also because it drew inspiration from Barth, whom I had continued to study pretty intensively, and because it constituted a call for doctrinal construction untroubled by epistemological scruple. The 'Yale school' – above all, Hans Frei's suggestions about how to read the history of Christology in the nineteenth century, and his exquisite probing of the ways in which theologians can allow general theory to submerge Christian self-description – offered a theoretically sophisticated and tough set of categories through which to develop a genealogy of modern theology.

Yet, however much I owed to Yale's 'post-liberalism', I remained dissatisfied. The dissatisfaction emerged initially over the interpretation of Barth. Neither Frei nor Lindbeck did sufficient justice to Barth's dogmatic concerns. They were attracted to aspects of his Christology, especially its use of biblical narrative, but they did not make very good sense of the dogmatics of Trinity and incarnation which undergird Barth's account of Jesus (to some extent, this was because they made the mistake of reading the *Church Dogmatics* backwards, starting with Barth's doctrine of reconciliation, and thereby missing the constitutive place of Barth's Trinitarian exposition of revelation). Moreover, the attributes of unsurpassability and irreducibility they tended to predicate on Christianity as a form of religious life or a sociolinguistic community, where Barth, by contrast, developed an immensely vigorous theological account of divine freedom. Accordingly, the centre of gravity in Lindbeck's *The Nature of Doctrine* and of Frei's later writings tended to be ecclesial, whereas for Barth it was always primarily trinitarian (and ecclesial, but only by derivation). I began to wonder if the problem I was encountering in the theology of Yale was that, *mirabile dictu*, it did not put dogmatics sufficiently to work, so that a (post-critical) notion of religion was assigned tasks which more properly ought to be assigned to a theology of resurrection or of the presence of the Holy Spirit. The result was that what seemed to many (especially to its critics) as a philosophically sophisticated Barthianism seemed to me, at least, to be more akin to Schleiermacher, though not the experiential Schleiermacher invented by hermeneutical theologians but Schleiermacher the practical theologian of the Christian community.

What I had stumbled into was something which I could have learned from Barth or many other theologians at the very beginning: the need to do dogmatics, and to do so with good humour, diligently and with a determination not to be troubled about having to swim against the stream, but rather to work away steadily at the given task as responsibly as possible. For me, this has meant busying myself with two principal spheres of work. One is that of becoming acquainted with the history of Christian theology, and coming to understand it as the history of the church: as *spiritual* history, as a history of attempts to articulate the Gospel, and not just as a lumber room full of opinions to be submitted to the critical scrutiny of 'valuers' and then auctioned off or discarded. The other task is that of trying to understand and think through the categories of classical dogmatics in their totality and their interrelations – to acquire a proper grasp of the architecture of dogmatics and to see its shape as the science of the Church's confession.

For much of the last ten years, work on these matters has been my major intellectual and spiritual preoccupation. When in the middle of that period I returned from Canada to teach in Oxford, and had once more to orient myself to British theology, I became more firmly convinced of the need to stick to my last, giving a distinctively theological account of the nature and ends of Christian theology and devoting my energy to the exposition of Christian dogmatics. I have found that commitment to this assignment has sometimes entailed a measure of academic isolation. In view of the widespread view that English language doctrinal theology is in a much healthier condition than it has been for many years, this isolation may seem odd. But as I read a great deal of contemporary systematic theology, I am struck by a sense that the centre of gravity is in the wrong place – usually it is heavily ecclesial, strongly invested in the Gospel as social and moral reality, overly invested in the language of habit, practice and virtue, underdetermined by a theology of divine aseity. It is not yet Ritschl; but, without a seriously operative eschatology, it has little protection against slipping into social and cultural immanentism (social Trinitarianism is already showing signs of drifting in that direction). And so I find myself at odds with those of my British colleagues who are more confident of the state of systematic theology: where they see an invigorated and invigorating discipline engaged in lively conversation in the academy, I tend to see a soft revisionism chastened by bits of Barth, or over-clever Anglo-Catholicism with precious little Christology, soteriology or pneumatology. I do not yet see much by way of positive dogmatics, though there are important exceptions that indicate good things to come.

II

How, then, do I now think of the task of theology and, more specifically, of dogmatic theology? Theology is an office in the Church of Jesus Christ. Whatever form there may be to the particular set of institutional arrangements in which it does its work, theology is properly undertaken in the sphere of the Church – in the sphere, that is, of the human community which is brought into being by the communicative, saving presence and activity of God. Theology is one of the activities of reason caught up by the miracle of the work of the triune God, a miracle which God himself makes manifest in his Word. This miracle, moreover, by virtue of the resurrection of Jesus Christ from the dead and in the sheerly creative power of the Holy Spirit, generates a new mode of common human life: the Church. To be a participant in that common human life is to be in the sphere in which God's limitless and supremely effective power is unleashed, extending into and renewing the totality of human life; moral, political and cultural, affective and intellectual. Reason, no less than body and conscience, stands under the sign of baptism. Theological reason is an exercise of the regenerate mind in the matter of the gospel of Jesus Christ that is at the heart of the Church's existence and calling.

The exercise of theological reason is an *office* in the Church. It is properly that to which the theologian is appointed and that for which the theologian is equipped; and, so appointed and equipped, the holder of the office of theologian is obliged to perform a specific task. Theology, to put it at its sharpest, is not a matter of 'free speech', if by 'free' is meant that which is unattached, undisciplined by the 'object' to which theology is by its very nature bound, namely the living communicative presence of God in Christ and in the Spirit's power. The activity of theological reason, rather, is undertaken as an act of deference; only in its deference to the given truth of its calling is it free. To speak in such terms is, of course, to go against the grain of some of the most influential modern accounts of the life of reason, according to which 'reason' is no more compatible with 'office' than it is with 'Church', since both office and Church, as mere domestic realities, are subject to the scrutiny of critical reason and can never be its founding conditions. If I have come to think otherwise, it is in part because I have profited from the critiques of the abstraction of reason from practice that have been mounted over the last century by thinkers as diverse as William James, Wittgenstein, Heidegger, George Grant, and many others. But it is more because I have gradually come to see that the Gospel itself must explicate the task of theological reason, since there is nothing that the Gospel does not explicate. Theological reason is as much a sphere of reconciliation, sanctification, prayer and Church as any other human undertaking.

As an office in the Church, theological reason works under the Church's tutelage, authority and protection. 'Church', of course, is to be understood spiritually, not merely naturally. It is to be understood, that is, as the sphere in which human fellowship is being sanctified by the Holy Spirit, and transformed into the communion of saints. Theological reason is under the Church's *tutelage* because it can only accomplish its office if it is instructed; only by immersing itself in the concepts, language and intellectual and spiritual habits of the *sanctorum communio* in all their variety can theology learn how to think and speak (what I missed in my theological education was, quite simply, catechism). Theological reason is under the Church's *authority* in the sense that, as a positive science, it is not at liberty to dispose of, reconstruct or otherwise manipulate its object. Reason and its judgments act according to law; law testifies to the shape of reality; authority is the exercise of power in order to quicken truthful action. Theological reason is thus under the authority of the

Church because (and only because) it is under the authority of truth. (This is why the exercise of Church authority over the activities of theological reason must only stem from the Church's deference to the claim of the Gospel, and must never be the prohibition of prophecy.) Theological reason is under the Church's *protection*, because what safeguards the truthfulness of theology is not, in the end, refined methodological awareness, a capacity for detachment or a confidence in its own superiority as an activity of transcendent rationality, but the confidence and fearfulness (here they are the same thing) with which it places itself in the hands of the one who is the Church's reconciler and Lord.

As an occupant of such an office, what does the theologian do? Most generally described, the task of theology is to take part in the common work of all the saints, that is, edifying the Church. Like all works of edification, it does this, not out of its own resources, but only insofar as it bears witness to the edifying presence of the risen Christ who through the Spirit speaks his Word, announcing his life-giving presence by which the Church is nourished and made to grow up into himself. The particular witness which theology bears is to the truth of the Gospel. Theology edifies by testifying to the Gospel's promise and claim, and so fulfils its evangelical call. More specifically, theology is that activity in the life of the community of the saints in which the Gospel is articulated as the norm of the Church's praise, confession and action (as liturgics, symbolics and ethics) and of its understanding of nature and human reality (as metaphysics and theology of culture).

At the centre of this articulation of the Gospel as the norm of the *sanctorum communio* are two fundamental tasks, namely exegesis and dogmatics. Of these tasks, exegesis is of supreme and supremely critical importance, because the instrument through which the risen Christ announces his Gospel is Holy Scripture. Exegesis, the attempt to hear what the Spirit says to the Churches, is that without which theological reason cannot even begin to discharge its office. To this primary activity of theological reason, dogmatics is complementary but strictly subordinate. One of the most disorderly developments in theology after the period of the magisterial reformers was the development of a notion of dogma as an improvement upon Holy Scripture – as the replacement of the informal and occasional language of Scripture by conceptual forms at once more clearly organized, better warranted and betraying a greater degree of sophistication. With that account of dogmatics I have become distinctly ill-at-ease, preferring a much more lightweight understanding of the dogmatic task. Dogmatics is about the business of setting forth 'commonplaces', a series of loosely organized proposals about the essential content of the witness of Holy Scripture, which serve to inform, guide and correct the Church's reading. Far from improving upon the scriptural material, dogmatics gives place to it. Like preaching (to which it is closely related) dogmatics is an attempt at reading, one whose goal is not 'interpretation' (transposing Scripture into some alien frame of reference or arguing in favour of its experiential viability) but simply hearing afresh the scriptural Gospel.

As I have come to try to reinvent for myself the office of theologian and the task of theology, in ways which seem to me fitting to the nature of the Christian confession, I have become aware how drastic (and drastically different) my conception has become. I have become aware, too, that to conceive of the office in this way leads me to say 'no' where many say 'yes', and to be cheerfully affirmative where many are hesitant. Most of all, I have become aware that the demands of the office, both intellectual and spiritual, are virtually unsupportable. For what must the theologian be? Holy, teachable, repentant, attentive to the confession of the Church, resistant to the temptation to treat it with irony or intellectual patronage, vigilant against the enticement to dissipate mind and spirit by attending to sources of fascination other than those held out by the Gospel. In short: the operation of theological reason is an exercise in mortification. But mortification is only possible and fruitful if it is generated by the vivifying power of the Spirit of Christ in which the Gospel is announced and its converting power made actual. And it is for this reason that theology must not only begin with but also be accompanied at every moment by prayer for the coming of the Spirit, in whose hands alone lie our minds and speeches.

Chapter 13

Method as Creative Fidelity:
Habitus and the *Sensus Communis*

Darren C. Marks

On Context and Method

A recent conversation with an Oxford graduate student struck at the heart of this text's preoccupation with method and context. The student, with a misguided sense that the theological task is prompted by an immediate interaction with Scripture alone, articulated the belief that any theological system that begins *only* by asking the question of its own historicity is doomed to be a theology of correlation. Once the straw man (or better yet 'bogeyman') of correlation was invoked, the conversation for him was closed; theology, in a misreading of Barth, vaccinated against crypto-liberalism in its method with a direct and immediate access to God by an appeal to Scripture, continues on its path, without being affected by culture or context and is as timeless and even immutable as its God. The problem with this quasi-mystical *Herrnhuter* referral of method to the 'strange world of the Bible' is the reduction of context and method to a simple equation. If what the student meant was that theological work is not bound to context by fate or necessity – that the job of the theologian was to criticize context from the vantage point of the Gospel understanding and therein the relativity of human constructions – then I would have little quarrel. Furthermore, if the student were asserting that the content of the Gospel, its object and subject's activity, gives theology its own unique referent and procedures, again there would be no contention. If this were the case, as in Barth (whom the student was using as a tacit reference), the theologian would feel completely free to maintain both a positive and a critical attitude to their theological situation. They, as Stephen C. Barton neatly summed up, exercise a 'creative fidelity' to the scriptural faith tradition, in which fidelity is a lesser co-agent, but a factor nonetheless, to a creative openness of the Spirit inspiring our interpretation and performing of that tradition.[1]

Turning more closely to Barth, theological history, both *our own* and the past history of others, is a 'theological task', the place wherein revelation intrudes into a wider and changeable cultural activity, which the Church is a part of, but also different from.[2] Contrary to some critics of Barth, this does not invoke a 'notwithstanding clause' of exemption or isolation of theology and the Church from a larger cultural conversation; rather, it requires a serious and sustained attention to the Gospel in the context of culture. It is not the assertion of a fideistic 'Christianness' over and against wider culture, but rather the attempt, humble and contingent, to find and articulate its own 'law of its own being' for each generation found within its 'own domain and from its own object'.[3] This means 'every period of the Church does in fact want to be understood as a period of the Church, that is, as a time of revelation, knowledge and confession of the one Christian faith; indeed, as *this* time of such revelation, knowledge and confession'.[4] This text attempts such an analysis, looking to see how each theologian attempted to find an answer in the Gospel to the context into which they found themselves. Moltmann's essay 'A lived theology' is an example of just such a theologian on an intensively personal level. The simple equation of correlation raised by the graduate student is far too reductionist, far too naïve and perhaps even timid or fearful. What we see in the essays is a confidence in the relevance of Christian 'creative fidelity'.

What each thinker raises is not merely a question of 'historicity' (*Geschichtlichkeit*), being their placement in time but how that historicity (or, to use Gerhard Sauter's apt term, 'context of discovery') is pierced by the more profound theological 'context of justification',[5] namely intrusion of the philanthropic God into the human situation. This is very different from the pietistic *Herrnhuter* view that the exclusive purview of revelation is the individual alone, thereby rendering revelation and the individual both as somehow suprahistorical or supracontextual (and by extension the Church itself). Instead, what is stressed is that all of human history and culture is capable of being understood as the place of, and transformed by, the action of God's intervention. The task of theology is to find, articulate and proclaim this intrusion of God. The hard break between 'dogmatic' and 'contextual' theologies is blurred in the above definition lest new 'ugly ditches' open up and swallow the theological task. Edward Farley and John Milbank's excellent reflection essays illustrate such a point. If the 'context of discovery', sociologies of knowledge, become the dominant partner then all one is left with is a reductionist and ironist position. Theologians merely baptize 'the battle lines of our world society'.[6] However, if the theological 'context of justification' is the dominant voice with its grounds 'given beforehand through God's gracious presence in the death and resurrection of Jesus Christ and that fix us upon the hope that awaits' then human experiences and contexts, even those hostile to God, 'are opened up to God's action'.[7]

As Gerhard Sauter notes, the difference between theological questions *exclusively* conditioned by time and situation and common or basic theological questions is that the latter are answered by a referral beyond the problems that provoked them. They are answered in the practice of the people of God who exist in the call, promise and hope of God, in whom *as the Church* the challenge of the day is overcome owing to the difference of God therein.[8] Context does not determine method; method, however, helps to heal context. Theology, therefore, is an ecclesiastical science and theology becomes the work of every Christian. Again, Sauter neatly sums up the situation:

> To exist theologically is to be a person under the promise and in the expectation of new life. Under this promise one is called, one is inserted into the situation that is opened up by God's condemning and saving judgment. One is inserted into the hidden history of Jesus Christ in the world. That *is* the living space in which our being human is 'located' and 'takes place'.[9]

This translocation or insertion of the person, a referral beyond context or even self-consciousness, to Christ (and thereby the Church) and that defining relation is what each of the essays attempted to explore. Each theologian sets the Gospel against his or her experience, allowing that experience to be reconfigured by the Gospel and the Gospel to answer questions therein. Whether context or faith *does* assume priority in method for each, history and scholarship will have to judge and debate, based on a larger *corpus*. What is clear, at least to me, is that each author attempts to answer questions raised by their context based on a perception of their theological existence in Christ.

Similarity in Dissimilarities

One purpose of this text was to discover whether there existed a core or barometer by which one could understand theological writings across the spectrum of denomination, age and geography. There are broad similarities in the work, such as the general consensus that Barth's break with the epistemological justification of theology as found in the nineteenth century is the proper way for theologians to proceed. Theologians no longer seem to be preoccupied, as Kathryn Tanner notes, with questions of justification. The possible exception to this is Keith Ward, and even here he is careful to note that he is working from within 'the distinctiveness of Christian faith . . . as given in the life, death and resurrection of Jesus'. Ward's theological project, he claims, is not 'revisionist', meaning altered so as to become intellectually credible, but *responsible* – meaning located in a wider context of God's soteriological actions in all of human history including other world faiths. Ward's project, if I read him correctly, is not concerned with making Christianity credible; it is concerned with making Christianity *honest* by reducing its propensity towards dogmatic absoluteness or exclusion in favour of a provisional and humble assent to God's presence in Christ and in the world writ large. This is a very different method than that which dominated the nineteenth century and the justification of theology in general. The most radically different essay of the set in Ward shares, at some basic level, the freedom of contemporary theology that theology need not be apologetic for its existence in the market place of ideas.

Another similarity found in the essays is that context is not merely the raising of problems as experienced by individuals to be referred to and answered by the Gospel's meaning, although that is a major motif in the work of James Cone, Wayne Meeks and Rosemary R. Ruether, but context is also the positive experience of thoughtful (dare we say Christian) communities and individuals. Context is not only to be overcome, but is also a boon to be thankful for. Gunton, McGrath, Webster and O'Collins are good examples of this positivity of context, having benefited from positive families, mentors and environments (even if those environs come from a privileged class or are an elite group such as Oxbridge, Kings College or the Gregorian Institute). Of course, almost all of the participants note the importance of their family and education in their development. This reintroduces the concept of consensus or theology as a collegial *habitus* noted in the Preface. Theology, above all disciplines, is still a mediaeval-style apprenticeship or 'discipleship' and needs to acknowledge that public character without fear of losing legitimacy in the academic environment.

The often-raised criticism that ecclesiastical consensus is a cul-de-sac for theology or a simple catechization is based on a mis-stress that somehow the *sensus communis* of the Church is akin to a public consensus of a society as found in sociopolitical forms. In the public sense, *consensus* is based on values derived from pure human convention. As such there is a contingency to their usage, a hesitation lest one's 'final vocabulary' becomes repressive, exclusionary or limiting. The theological usage of *consensus*, as found throughout this work, is already invested with an intrinsic hesitancy due to the nature of its common object of worship. Christian theology, rather than self-assured catechization, assumes that its God is the hidden and revealed God of the cross; that in listening one learns to be a servant, patiently and prayerfully to expect God yet also to expect human sinfulness and error. This is a dialectical problem; Christian theology cannot help, owing to its subject and object, but to assert and to claim itself as a universal science in its scope and yet it must remain humble and reticent in its judgments. The faithful scriptural tradition as the *sensus communis* is the spine of this reflection. Christian theology, however, is also mindful that the Church is not God, ecclesiology not Christology and that there is provisionality in its judgments. The *sensus communis* as an eschatological community, awaiting redemption, keeps the *communio* from becoming institutionalized or conflated with Churchly forms. In the context of the essays, each thinker cites a litany of examples – learned colleagues or teachers and faithful 'simple' Christians – who have taught the value of such a notion of communal and humble understanding of Christian faith. Furthermore, this 'teaching' was not only in the form of what is positive, but often, as indicated above in Cone, Meeks, Moltmann and Ruether, is found in the form of what was decidedly missing from a common sense of Christian truth that *should* be manifest in the communion of the faithful.

The 'State of the Union'

What, then, can be said from this collection of essays across a spectrum of situations? Perhaps the most important statement is the most obvious. Theology is alive and well, hopeful that it serves its Church and thereby its object by seeking to find 'God' in our theological existence today in a method of 'creative fidelity'. Its answers, Milbank's 'last of the last', is this expectation of a fusion of 'human and divine rhetoric' being nothing more, returning to Barth, than an expectation of 'theological existence today'.

Notes

1   Stephen C. Barton (2001), 'The Epistles and Christian Ethics', in R. Gill (ed.), *Cambridge Companion to Christian Ethics*, Cambridge: Cambridge University Press, p.71. For all that follows I am indebted to Prof J. Webster's patient teaching. Any misunderstanding of Barth, however, remains mine.
2   The locus of Barth's understanding of theological history is his introduction in *Protestant Theology in the Nineteenth Century*. Of particular note is Barth's twofold claim. First is that reflection on Church history is a reflection on one holy apostolic Church, meaning we are not in a position of 'better' judgment by being further down the historical line or that we are different from those who struggled before us to be faithful. Barth's claim 'Over and above the differences . . . a unity can continually be seen, a unity of perplexity and disquiet, but also a unity of richness and hope, which in the end binds us to the theologians of the past', must be rediscovered for *theological* or *church* history without falling prey to historicism. The second claim follows from the first, this being that the task of theology is its concern with its subject, asking what is 'theological existence today' by looking to its subject and attending to the Gospel (Karl Barth (1972), *Protestant Thought in the Nineteenth Century: Its Background and History*, trans. B. Cozens and J. Bowden, London: SCM, p.27).
3   Karl Barth (1963), *Evangelical Theology: an Introduction*, trans. G. Foley, London: Nicolson, p.15.
4   Barth, *Protestant Thought*, p.27.
5   Gerhard Sauter (1996), 'Eschatological Rationality', *Eschatological Rationality*, Grand Rapids: Eerdman, pp.171–83. Professor Sauter was to be included in this volume and it is only fitting that some of his thought should be mentioned in the volume, if only as a stimulus to my own. I am grateful for his friendship and stimulus in this area.
6   Sauter, p.187.
7   Ibid.
8   See Sauter's notion of a dynamic consensus of faith, *Eschatological Rationality*, pp.188–92.
9   Sauter, p.198.

Index

Fascism and the Right in Europe, 1919–1945

Pearson Education Limited
Edinburgh Gate
Harlow
Essex CM20 2JE
England
and Associated Companies throughout the world.

Visit us on the World Wide Web at:
www.pearsoned.co.uk

First published 2000

ISBN 978-0-582-07021-9

British Library Cataloguing-in-Publication Data
A catalogue record for this book is
available from the British Library

Library of Congress Cataloging-in-Publication Data
A catalog record for this book is available from the Library of Congress

Transferred to Digital Print on Demand 2011

Set by 7 in 10/12 Sabon Roman
Printed and bound by CPI Group (UK) Ltd, Croydon, CR0 4YY

SEMINAR STUDIES IN HISTORY

Fascism and the Right in Europ 1919–1945

MARTIN BLINKHORN

Longman

An imprint of **Pearson Education**

Harlow, England · London · New York · Reading, Massachusetts · San Francisco · Toronto · Do
Tokyo · Singapore · Hong Kong · Seoul · Taipei · Cape Town · Madrid · Mexico City · Amsterdar

For Irene

CONTENTS